WINTER SEASON

A Women's Bible Study in Ecclesiastes

FOR EVERYTHING THERE IS A SEASON,
A TIME FOR EVERY MATTER UNDER HEAVEN.
ECCLESIASTES 3:1

DENISE GLENN

Published by Kardo International Ministries

Copyright ©2020 Denise Glenn

All rights reserved. No part of this publication may be reproduced or transmitted in any form or by any means, electronic or mechanical, including photocopy, recording, or any information storage and retrieval system without written permission by the author and publisher. Requests for permission should be emailed to: info@kardo.org

Unless otherwise noted, Scripture quotations are from the ESV® Bible (The Holy Bible, English Standard Version®), copyright © 2001 by Crossway Bibles, a publishing ministry of Good News Publishers. Used by permission. All rights reserved.

To order additional copies:
Visit www.kardo.org or call 1-888-272-6972

Cover Design by Delynn Halloran
of Delynn Photography at delynnphotography.com

Cover image used by permission from photographer, John Clay

Book Design by Kristan King

Printed in the United States of America

TO OUR GRANDCHILDREN

Rachel
Susannah
Ben
Edi
Samantha
Bekah
Anna
Leia
Will
Samuel

May God give you wisdom all your days, and may you remember your Creator in the days of your youth. May He bless you and keep you and use you for His glory to reach the nations. You are our heart and our joy, our hope for future generations. We love you with all our hearts. We did our best to make an impact on our generation. Now it's your turn to make an impact on yours.

ACKNOWLEDGMENTS

TO DAVID GLENN
Thank you to my wonderful husband whose prayers and hours of research helped to form this Bible study. We worked side by side on the women's and men's books in constant collaboration. When one became tired and discouraged, the other bolstered the team until, at last, we finished the manuscript. I cannot imagine life without his faithful prayers, his companionship in ministry, and the fun we have on a daily basis just doing life together.

TO STEPHANIE GLENN OTTOSEN
I want to thank our daughter, Stephanie, for untold hours she poured into this project, not only as a professional editor but also as a continual encourager every step of the way. Steph is an incredible writer in her own right and lent her God-given ability join me in producing this book. This project brought us together in an even closer bond as mother and daughter, and I'll be forever grateful.

TO EDI AND SAMANTHA OTTOSEN
A big thank you goes out to my lovely granddaughters who gave their input to the design and content of this book. As teenagers they have a unique perspective, and I love that they invested time and energy in bringing this book to life.

TO KRISTAN KING
Many thanks to Kristan for her beautiful design for this book. Her attention to detail and her artistic eye made the study of Ecclesiastes easy to navigate and pretty to look at as well. I so appreciate her sweet attitude and diligence in her work.

TO DELYNN HALLORAN
A huge thanks to Delynn for once again designing the cover of this book. This is our ninth collaboration for the covers of our books, and I am so grateful that God brought us together many years ago to work together to create Bible studies for women. What a joy and privilege to work with Delynn again.

TO JOHN CLAY
We are so grateful to Mr. Clay for his generosity in granting permission for us to use his beautiful blue jay photograph for the cover of this book.

TO LINDA BRADSHAW AND PAM SANCHEZ
Linda and Pam dedicated themselves to proofread this book, and that meant many hours of reading and checking and then checking again. I am indebted to both Linda and Pam for their wonderful skills and untiring dedication to making sure we have the best book possible.

INTRODUCTION TO WINTER SEASON

In June 2015, I was plunged into a Winter Season in the span of a five-minute phone call. My 90-year-old mother had a medical crisis, and she and my sister were heading to the emergency room. Death was certain without surgery; but even with it, the doctors weren't sure she would survive. Up to this point, my elderly parents were both living and in good health—they lived on their own at home, and my father was still exercising at his gym five days a week! That one phone call changed everything. Suddenly, my three sisters and I were facing the possibility of losing our mother, who also happened to be the caretaker of my father, whose memory and mental function were fading.

By God's grace, my mother lived through the surgery that spared her, but life was never the same again. That one phone call began a five-year journey that included her recovering at a rehabilitation-nursing home, moving our dad into the same place to be with her, and taking on the total responsibility of their care. During that time, we also sold the house they'd lived in for 40 years and finally said goodbye to them 13 months apart when God took them to His heavenly home. I just said in one paragraph what took me to the darkest place I'd ever been.

For me, the Winter Season has been a time of grief and loss, of feeling my world as I knew it turned upside down. But it's not like life came to a stop so that I could deal with all of these heavy things. I'm blessed to live near my three daughters, their husbands and our 10 grandchildren, which means I was trying to balance being present in their lives, continuing to speak and travel with Kardo Ministries and helping take care of my ailing parents who lived a four-hour drive away. It was a lot.

I've just begun to come out of the fog of those years, and I can say that I learned so much from that time. Some things I wouldn't change, such as the way my sisters and I honored and cared for our parents. But others, such as the way I cared for myself, I would do differently.

I wasn't necessarily planning to write another book, but the Lord laid this message on my heart; and I want to share the good news with you that joy is possible on the other side and even in the midst of your Winter Season. Your Winter Season might look very different from mine, but going through challenging circumstances happens to everyone. Winter Season might be brought on by a sudden change like a new job or a new baby, a job loss or retirement, a season with a prodigal child or elderly parents. A death or divorce, a sudden devastating illness, or a sin that destroys a life and all the people around them can send you into the Winter Season. It is a season that is especially hard for you, and you need answers. Some people seem to live their lives in Winter Season, never turning the corner to joy and peace.

What we need for the Winter Season is wisdom to get through the rough patches into a place of stability and security. We need answers to life's big questions. We want to understand when life's not fair, when the good guy doesn't win. We long for God to speak to us when we're broken-hearted, disillusioned, grieving and torn. What do the wise men say about our situation? What we need in the Winter Season is the book of Ecclesiastes. Ecclesiastes is a book that faces harsh reality, raw emotion and deep truth head on. I don't know about you, but that's exactly what I need.

What people are saying about Winter Season...

♦ *When I think of reading Ecclesiastes, I typically feel the need to steel myself for an unpleasant reality check, but* Winter Season *was a refreshing take on a book that turns out to be full of goodness and wisdom. It revealed to me that the ultimate goal for ourselves and our children should not be to gain riches or honor, because Solomon had all that and yet it did not satisfy him. Instead, I'm learning to trust God more, knowing that all my striving is in vain outside of God's plans for me.*

♦ Winter Season *could not have come at a more strategic time in my life. While my earthly father was being called home by our heavenly Father, this study held my hand and guided me through my very own "Winter Season" with Scripture and personal life experiences. What a blessing!*

♦ *There is so much to be gained from this study from Ecclesiastes, no matter what stage of life you find yourself. But, for me, it was very timely as my husband and I entered a new phase of life with his retirement.*

WINTER SEASON:
A WOMEN'S BIBLE STUDY IN ECCLESIASTES
TABLE OF CONTENTS

WEEK 1: WHO WAS THE WISEST MAN IN THE WORLD, AND WHY SHOULD I TRUST HIM?
Ecclesiastes 1:1-11   **Page 1**

In this first week of study, we'll discover the back story about Solomon, the author of Ecclesiastes, and why he is qualified to give us the wisdom we need. The wisest and wealthiest man who's ever lived knows that "all is vanity" without the right perspective.

WEEK 2: WHAT IS THE BEST WAY TO LIVE MY LIFE?
Ecclesiastes 1:12-2:26   **Page 39**

Solomon searches for the best way to spend our few years on earth. He pursues intellect, pleasure, and work to the extreme and then takes a look at his legacy to leave behind. What's left is ultimately meaningless…unless we choose a different path.

WEEK 3: WHAT TIME IS IT? PART 1
Ecclesiastes 3:1-3   **Page 75**

Solomon takes a bird's eye view of life and teaches about the different seasons of time that we all experience, whether we are ready for them or not. We'll discover why each distinct season has something to teach us.

WEEK 4: WHAT TIME IS IT? PART 2
Ecclesiastes 3:4-22   **Page 115**

Solomon continues his teaching on the seasons of life and why each is important in bringing wholeness and balance to our lives.

WEEK 5: HOW SHOULD I MANAGE MY RESOURCES AND PREPARE MY HEIRS?
Ecclesiastes 4-6   **Page 151**

Solomon gives us wisdom for leaving a legacy and speaks to us about issues such as how to use our words, how to use our money, and how to prepare our heirs before we're gone.

WEEK 6: WHEN LIFE IS SHORT, HOW CAN I MAKE THE MOST OF IT?
Ecclesiastes 7-9   **Page 187**

Solomon digs into the difficult times in our lives and offers guidance for dealing with suffering, keeping life in balance, handling authority figures and facing our mortality. But it doesn't end there!

WEEK 7: WHAT BRINGS ULTIMATE MEANING TO LIFE?
Ecclesiastes 10-12   **Page 219**

Solomon's final words help us avoid foolish pitfalls and pursue lifelong wisdom. He tells us how to live productive lives, how to handle the aging process with grace, and how to put the past behind us. He ends with a final punch line that will change our lives forever!

BIBLE STUDY NOTES

WEEK 1
WHO WAS THE WISEST MAN IN THE WORLD, AND WHY SHOULD I TRUST HIM?

A Personal Message to You from Solomon

I have a lot to tell you. I've lived through so much and learned more than you can imagine. I've seen enough of life to be able to steer you away from the pitfalls and toward the path of joy and peace. Please listen to me. I don't want you to make the same mistakes I did. I've taken the time to write down the things I want to leave with you before I'm gone. I hope you're paying attention. I wrote Proverbs as a first course, but now I want to share with you something more advanced, more like a graduate course in wisdom. That's why I wrote Ecclesiastes. But first, you need to know who I am.

THE PREACHER

Lord Jesus, I long to know the truth that will set me free in this season and time of my life. Show me the way. Lead me with Your wisdom, Your mind and Your heart. I love You and trust You, Jesus. It is in Your matchless name I pray, Amen.

We often learn the best by experience. It was like that for me, as I had to experience a Winter Season before I could ever really understand it and certainly before I could ever write a book about it. Caring for my elderly parents, facing their deaths, having an adult daughter with a chronic illness, and dealing with my own aging issues have all thrust me into a Winter Season. I knew I needed wisdom that I didn't have for this intense season of life. I turned to the book of Ecclesiastes to explore Solomon's Winter Season and find direction.

Just as I wrote the story of Ruth and Levi in one of my previous Bible studies, *Restore My Heart*, I wanted to tell a fictional story in this book that would flesh out the truths of Ecclesiastes in a practical way. Allow me to introduce you to the Page family.

THE PAGE SISTERS—all five of them—had grown up in a home overflowing with love, support and encouragement. Their parents took them to church from the time they were babies, and in time each one of them decided that they would accept the love of Jesus Christ and follow Him all of their lives. They took their faith as seriously as their parents did. But they were very different; and with personalities and gifts that ranged the spectrum, they each faced challenges that, at this juncture of their lives, brought them to their knees. Each of them was in a Winter Season of their own that came from different circumstances.

ABIGAIL, THE ELDEST, was married to John, the head of their big, bustling, noisy family. She had mountains of energy; and it was a good thing, too, since she and John owned and ran a restaurant, taught a Bible study at church and had a revolving door of high school and college-aged students in their home. Life was very full, in a good way. But some days it was just too much. Abby was also the primary caregiver for Mom and Dad, and it felt like everyone expected her to keep things running for both her own family and her parents.

DAPHNE'S life took a turn she would have never expected when her husband, Richard, left her for a younger woman. As if that weren't bad enough, he had actually married her! Daphne should now be heading toward retirement and enjoying time with her husband, but she was alone, single and in financial straits. This wasn't the way she'd imagined her life, but she trusted that God would carry her through.

LOVELY, ARTSY CELINA was the middle daughter who was the easiest to get along with. She was the fun aunt to all the nieces and nephews and had the ability to connect at a heart level with everyone around her. If only she was as good with money as she was with people! Celina always struggled to pay the bills with her equally flighty but lovable husband, Paul. Unfortunately, now they realized that their meager retirement savings weren't going to be enough and even though they were both really ready to stop working, they couldn't for several more years.

ELIZABETH had been struggling with her health for months. Still she was the steady, sweet one who served both her family and the church. She helped her sisters and parents with practical things like their taxes, served in the church's international ministry, and prayed faithfully on the church prayer team. In spite of her illness and with the support of Stephen, her beloved husband of many years, she was able to continue most of her family and ministry obligations. Then suddenly, Stephen had a stroke; and everything changed. Elizabeth became his caregiver and for several years, poured herself into his care until the day the Lord took Stephen home. Now, while she was left alone to face her own illness, she drew strength and life from the Lord like never before.

Madeline was the baby of the family by many years, arriving long after the others were already in school. Although as the darling of the family she could have been selfish and spoiled, she was the opposite. Madeline and her husband, Luke, were missionaries in Asia, caring, giving, and surrendering their lives in service. She knew they were where God had called them to be, but daily living in a foreign environment and possibly facing a new assignment that would keep them away from extended family even longer, took her to a Winter Season of her own.

Winter Season is a Bible study on Ecclesiastes, not for a particular age person but for a season of life. Ecclesiastes is a piece of wisdom literature in the heart of the Bible that speaks to the deep places in the heart about big issues. It's a book that allows us to step outside our daily lives, to "go up 30,000 feet" and look down at what's really important. For those going through a difficult season of loss or change, Ecclesiastes will help you work through it. For those hungry to learn from the wisest man who ever lived, this book will chart your path. For those asking big questions about life, Ecclesiastes explores them with you and leads you to the truth. For first-world mature adults either nearing retirement or enjoying it, this book is critical.

Solomon is an experienced guide who has tested the waters and knows his way to steer us clear of the obstacles. In his philosophical, sometimes poetic way, he brings us the truth about the most serious issues in life—money, control, aging, legacy, death, trials, sex (or lack of it), joy, wisdom, and faith. In eras past, Ecclesiastes was called a "dangerous book," and some even now say it's a "downer." But I beg to differ! Solomon does look at life realistically, seeing all the brokenness in our world, but Ecclesiastes is a book full of wisdom and insight from a wise man ready to share the secrets of life.

Ecclesiastes will take us on a journey where we will see life from both the messy underside of the tapestry and the finished topside when all is completed in God's eternal plan. There will be black threads woven throughout; but when we see it from God's perspective, we see those threads just outline the beautiful design God is making of our lives. Ecclesiastes won't read like a novel. It isn't meant to be read from beginning to end, easily digested and set aside. When read in a single sitting, Ecclesiastes seems to meander in circles and lack organization. Next to the fascinating stories of the Old and New Testaments, it lacks a coherently unfolding story. No, this book is organized in a way far different from a modern novel or newspaper. And that's part of its unique power and challenge.

Ecclesiastes is meant to be read and studied verse by verse, a little section at a time, contemplated and the wisdom absorbed and applied. As we study, you'll want to zoom in on one or two verses each day that speak to you and where you are right now. But first, we need to know who wrote this book and why you can trust that he knows what he's talking about.

Read Ecclesiastes 1:1.
The words of the Preacher, the son of David, king in Jerusalem. (ESV)

Who is the probable writer of Ecclesiastes?

What do we learn about this man?

The writer of Ecclesiastes identifies himself as the "Preacher" (ESV) and "Teacher" (NIV). The Hebrew word is *koheleth*.[1] It means "assembler," "lecturer" or "preacher." He is *koheleth*, the one who has gone astray and gathered or "assembled" back to God. He is *koheleth*, the one who wrote to bring the lost sheep back to the shepherd by preaching a sermon. The traditional view, including that of noted biblical scholar Matthew Henry, is that this book is authored by Solomon, as stated in verse one, and that he is "the son of David, king in Jerusalem."[2]

Solomon, whose name means "peace," used a pen name instead of writing under his own name as he did in Proverbs and Song of Solomon because, at the end of his life, he didn't bring peace to the kingdom, nor to himself, but trouble. Solomon, the Teacher or Preacher, gives a long sermon in the book of Ecclesiastes to show us that the things of this world, in the end, are vanity and will not make us happy. Solomon ends the sermon with a simple solution to this dilemma that will lead us to joy. So, who was Solomon, and why should we listen to him?

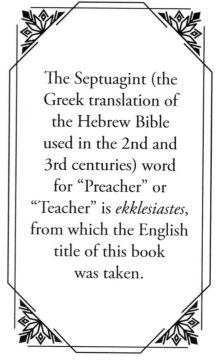

The Septuagint (the Greek translation of the Hebrew Bible used in the 2nd and 3rd centuries) word for "Preacher" or "Teacher" is *ekklesiastes*, from which the English title of this book was taken.

Read the following passages from II Samuel 11:2-12:25 about Solomon's birth and summarize the story from the following passages.

²David arose from his couch and was walking on the roof of the king's house, that he saw from the roof a woman bathing; and the woman was very beautiful. ³And David sent and inquired about the woman. And one said, "Is not this Bathsheba, the daughter of Eliam, the wife of Uriah the Hittite?" ⁴So David sent messengers and took her, and she came to him, and he lay with her.

(Now she had been purifying herself from her uncleanness.) Then she returned to her house. ⁵And the woman conceived, and she sent and told David, "I am pregnant."

(From Nathan the Prophet) 12:9 Why have you despised the word of the LORD, to do what is evil in his sight? You have struck down Uriah the Hittite with the sword and have taken his wife to be your wife and have killed him with the sword of the Ammonites. ¹⁰Now therefore the sword shall never depart from your house, because you have despised me and have taken the wife of Uriah the Hittite to be your wife.'

¹⁵And the Lord afflicted the child that Uriah's wife bore to David, and he became sick.

(King David) ²³But now he is dead. Why should I fast? Can I bring him back again? I shall go to him, but he will not return to me." ²⁴Then David comforted his wife, Bathsheba, and went in to her and lay with her, and she bore a son, and he called his name Solomon. And the Lord loved him ²⁵and sent a message by Nathan the prophet. So, he called his name Jedidiah, because of the Lord.

Who was Solomon's mother?

What were the circumstances of his birth?

WEEK 1: DAY 1

Google the meaning of the names "Solomon" and "Jedidiah" and write the definitions here.

Why were those names given to this baby?

✳ What did you learn that helps you understand the man Solomon became?

> Throughout the book you will see a snowflake beside some of the questions. These are for discussion with your group.

Solomon, born to King David and Bathsheba after they married, was a legitimate son. For David and Bathsheba, who lost the child of their adultery before their marriage, Solomon must have represented a second chance, redemption, and God's forgiveness. He was God's gift to them and represented resurrection of their marriage, David's reign, and the cleansing of the kingdom. Their first son embodied their sin. Their second son personified their restoration. They named him Solomon, from *shalom*, meaning "peace." David had made peace with God about his sin. When Nathan, the prophet, came to see the baby, he brought a blessing from God for the boy and called him Jedidiah, "beloved of God" or "friend of God." God had his hand on Solomon's life from the beginning.

[1]*Strong's Exhaustive Concordance of the Bible,* Hebrew Number 6953, biblehub.com.

[2]*Commentary on the Whole Bible by Matthew Henry,* 1961, Zondervan Publishing House, p. 791-792.

A Bit of Wisdom

Like King David, we all have past sins and regrets. Take some time today to forgive yourself of those poor choices. It's a first step to the next chapter of your life. Until you give to God all those things that haunt your thoughts and nag at the corners of your mind, you'll never be free to be the person you can be in Him.

These are old tricks, but they work. Take out a sheet of paper and write down the details of your past that still bother you today—mistakes, outright sins, foolish decisions that caused pain, harm or just inconvenience. Thoughts that continue to go around and around in your mind, never finding resolution because you can't go back in time and re-do any of them. Put them on paper and ask God to forgive you for each one and for the consequences others had to pay because of them. Ask Him to wash you clean, heal and restore you. Then, in a safe place, burn or shred that paper and throw it away. Now, receive God's forgiveness by celebrating. Maybe your celebration will just be to walk in the sunshine or take a long soaking bath. Maybe you'll go to dinner with your loved one. Take a moment to mark the event when you receive God's restoration.

THE CHOSEN ONE — Day 2

Lord Jesus, thank You for choosing me to be in Your family. Thank You for the plan You have designed for my life. Lord, I want to walk in Your plan alone. Here is my life. Use me. Fill me. Send me. In the name of Jesus, I pray. Amen.

DAPHNE was lonely. Richard's abrupt departure from their marriage in favor of a younger woman had left her angry, hurt, feeling inadequate and ugly both inside and out. She needed wisdom to know how to move forward. For months that seemed like years, she'd been stuck in never-ending cycles of self-reproach, self-hatred, and searing anger toward Richard for his traitorous infidelity. How dare he! Well, today, she decided, would be a different day. She was finished with the pity party and ready for a fresh start. Since it was Saturday, she was in her robe and slippers when she curled up in her big chair with coffee in hand and began to read Ecclesiastes. While it seemed an unlikely choice of reading material to lift her spirits, the Lord directed her to this book that would help her through this Winter Season in her life.

She decided to begin learning more about Solomon, the author of the book. Why did he write it and what were his credentials that gave him the ability to give her wisdom? In her research, she found out that David, his father, had many sons. He had six sons by different wives before Solomon was even born. Shouldn't they have succeeded David to the throne of Israel instead of Solomon?

Read II Samuel 3:2-5.
²And sons were born to David at Hebron: his firstborn was Amnon, of Ahinoam of Jezreel; ³and his second, Chileab, of Abigail the widow of Nabal of Carmel; and the third, Absalom the son of Maacah the daughter of Talmai king of Geshur; ⁴and the fourth, Adonijah the son of Haggith; and the fifth, Shephatiah the son of Abital; ⁵and the sixth, Ithream, of Eglah, David's wife. These were born to David in Hebron.

Who was the firstborn of King David, the rightful heir to his throne and why was he disqualified? (See II Samuel 13:1-22.)

Why was another older brother of Solomon disqualified from being king? (Read the story in II Samuel 15:1-12, 16:15-23, 18:10-15.)

What was the likelihood of Solomon becoming king because of his birth order?

David's first six sons were each born of a different mother. They would all have been in line for the throne before Solomon. The first son of David and Bathsheba, David's seventh son, died in infancy. Solomon was the eighth son of David, who was himself, the eighth son of his father, Jesse. Only God could ordain an eighth son of an eighth son to be the king of Israel.

Read I Kings 1:32-35.
³²King David said, "Call to me Zadok the priest, Nathan the prophet, and Benaiah the son of Jehoiada." So they came before the king. ³³And the king said to them, "Take with you the servants of your lord and have Solomon my son ride on my own mule, and bring him down to Gihon. ³⁴And let Zadok the priest and Nathan the prophet there anoint him king over Israel. Then blow the trumpet and say, 'Long live King Solomon!' ³⁵You shall then come up after him, and he shall come and sit on my throne, for he shall be king in my place. And I have appointed him to be ruler over Israel and over Judah."

How was Solomon crowned king?

Why was there a question about his succession to the throne? (I Kings 1:1-53.)

Read I Chronicles 28:1-7 to discover God's plan for Solomon's kingship.

¹David assembled at Jerusalem all the officials of Israel, the officials of the tribes, the officers of the divisions that served the king, the commanders of thousands, the commanders of hundreds, the stewards of all the property and livestock of the king and his sons, together with the palace officials, the mighty men and all the seasoned warriors. ²Then King David rose to his feet and said: "Hear me, my brothers and my people. I had it in my heart to build a house of rest for the ark of the covenant of the LORD and for the footstool of our God, and I made preparations for building. ³But God said to me, 'You may not build a house for my name, for you are a man of war and have shed blood.'

⁴Yet the LORD God of Israel chose me from all my father's house to be king over Israel forever. For he chose Judah as leader, and in the house of Judah my father's house, and among my father's sons he took pleasure in me to make me king over all Israel. ⁵And of all my sons (for the LORD has given me many sons) he has chosen Solomon my son to sit on the throne of the kingdom of the LORD over Israel. ⁶He said to me, 'It is Solomon your son who shall build my house and my courts, for I have chosen him to be my son, and I will be his father. ⁷I will establish his kingdom forever if he continues strong in keeping my commandments and my rules, as he is today.'

Who appointed Solomon to be king of Israel according to verse 5?

✺ What was the special relationship between Solomon and God as stated in verse 6?

✺ What was the condition God placed on Solomon's reign being firmly established?

Solomon was specifically chosen by God to be king after David. He ascended the throne of Israel, with a task appointed by both his earthly father and heavenly Father. David charged his son to observe God's commandments with a whole heart and a willing mind. David knew what he was talking about. His sin had cost him dearly. He wanted better for this son of promise. David gave to Solomon the wisdom he had acquired by sitting at the feet of the Lord but also by making terrible mistakes. He knew by experience that "the Lord searches all hearts and understands every intent of the thoughts."

In I Chronicles 28:7, David repeats God's words in the hearing of all Israel and to his son, "I will establish his kingdom forever if…

_____

_____

✺ What did you learn today from David about counseling your children, even adult children and grandchildren?

What message do you want to communicate with your kids from what you have learned through the experiences of your life?

A Bit of Wisdom

Pray for your children and grandchildren to make wise choices today, this week, and this year. Your prayer might sound something like this:

"Lord Jesus, thank You for my beautiful children. You created them wonderfully and uniquely for Your purpose. Now today, I lift them up to You, asking You to give them the gift of wisdom in making decisions. I am asking according to James 1:5-6, where Your word says, "if any of you lacks wisdom, let him ask of God, who gives to all men generously and without reproach and it will be given to him."

So, Lord, pour out Your wisdom into their hearts and minds. Strip away fear and unbelief. Give them unusual discernment before they make final decisions. I entrust my children into Your hands, knowing that the plans You have for them are to prosper them and not to harm them, to give them a hope and a future. I ask all this in the powerful name of Jesus, the name above every other name. Amen."

Sir Isaac Newton, Albert Einstein & Stephen Hawking Rolled Into One

Day 3

Heavenly Father, I come today before You to adore and bless Your name. You are God of all gods and Lord over all things in heaven and earth. I praise You, O God. Thank You for every blessing You have given to me. I am so grateful for every good and perfect gift. Today I am counting my blessings. I love You, Lord. Amen.

THE YOUNGEST SISTER, MADELINE, and her husband, Luke, had some big decisions to make in their ministry. They were asked to take a new assignment, but it wouldn't be easy. Not only was the assignment truly God-sized, way outside their scope, but it was far from home. With aging parents and young adult children, the answer wasn't going to be easy, whether they accepted or rejected the offer. They needed to be wiser than ever. They both had seminary degrees, but they didn't need a lot of heavy theology tonight. They needed a clear word of wisdom from the Lord.

Read I Chronicles 28:10-12 and I Chronicles 29:1-3.
¹⁰Be careful now, for the Lord has chosen you to build a house for the sanctuary; be strong and do it." ¹¹Then David gave Solomon his son the plan of the vestibule of the temple, and of its houses, its treasuries, its upper rooms, and its inner chambers, and of the room for the mercy seat; ¹²and the plan of all that he had in mind for the courts of the house of the Lord, all the surrounding chambers, the treasuries of the house of God, and the treasuries for dedicated gifts;

29:1 And David the king said to all the assembly, "Solomon my son, whom alone God has chosen, is young and inexperienced, and the work is great, for the palace will not be for man but for the LORD God. ²So I have provided for the house of my God, so far as I was able, the gold for the things of gold, the silver for the things of silver, and the bronze for the things of bronze, the iron for the things of iron, and wood for the things of wood, besides great quantities of onyx and stones for setting, antimony, colored stones, all sorts of precious stones and marble. ³Moreover, in addition to all that I have provided for the holy house, I have a treasure of my own of gold and silver, and because of my devotion to the house of my God I give it to the house of my God:

What was the legacy David left to Solomon before he died?

Solomon was to build a spectacular temple for the worship of God. King David had dreamed of building this temple, but that privilege was given to his son. So, David transferred all the plans and provisions for the task, carefully explaining to Solomon everything in his heart for this beautiful building. David recognized his place in history and that of his son. He did his part willingly and happily passed the baton. It was up to Solomon to have courage and take action to get it done.

He must have been daunted by such big shoes to fill as those of his father, David, and such an overwhelming responsibility to not only lead Israel as king but to oversee the building of a permanent, magnificent place for offering sacrifices to God.

Read I Kings 3:3-5.
³Solomon loved the LORD, walking in the statutes of David his father, only he sacrificed and made offerings at the high places. ⁴And the king went to Gibeon to sacrifice there, for that was the great high place. Solomon used to offer a thousand burnt offerings on that altar. ⁵At Gibeon the LORD appeared to Solomon in a dream by night, and God said, **"Ask what I shall give you."**

Describe Solomon's relationship with God.

How did Solomon prove his zeal for loving and worshiping God?

Did he worship God in the same place as David his father? Why or why not?

What did God say to Solomon?

How did Jesus repeat that in Matthew 7:7, 8?

What do you want to ask of God today?

Solomon really loved the Lord God and demonstrated that love by 1000 sacrifices on the altar. He chose to worship at the high place instead of at the tabernacle before the ark of the covenant. Was this a first step away from worshiping the one true God? He had not yet received his wisdom and was young and inexperienced. God gave him grace and accepted his sacrifice without judgment. And He asked Solomon the million-dollar question that any man would envy. God asked him what he wanted. Solomon could literally ask for anything! Here is his interesting reply to God.

Read I Kings 3:6-9.

⁶And Solomon said, "You have shown great and steadfast love to your servant David my father, because he walked before you in faithfulness, in righteousness, and in uprightness of heart toward you. And you have kept for him this great and steadfast love and have given him a son to sit on his throne this day. ⁷And now, O LORD my God, you have made your servant king in place of David my father, although I am but a little child. I do not know how to go out or come in. ⁸And your servant is in the midst of your people whom you have chosen, a great people, too many to be numbered or counted for multitude. ⁹Give your servant therefore an understanding mind to govern your people, that I may discern between good and evil, for who is able to govern this your great people?"

What did Solomon ask of God?

What was Solomon's attitude toward God?

Read I Kings 3:10-14 to discover God's answer in His dialogue with Solomon.

¹⁰It pleased the Lord that Solomon had asked this. ¹¹And God said to him, "Because you have asked this, and have not asked for yourself long life or riches or the life of your enemies, but have asked for yourself understanding to discern what is right, ¹²behold, I now do according to your word. Behold, I give you a wise and discerning mind, so that none like you has been before you and none like you shall arise after you. ¹³I give you also what you have not asked, both riches and honor, so that no other king shall compare with you, all your days. ¹⁴And if you will walk in my ways, keeping my statutes and my commandments, as your father David walked, then I will lengthen your days."

What was God's answer to Solomon?

God appeared to him in a dream and asked Solomon what he wished for as a new king. Humbled, he asked God for discernment and wisdom, and God was so pleased with his unselfish request that he granted him both wisdom and incredible wealth and if Solomon was obedient to God's commands, he would be granted a long life. God lavished upon this boy of David's a heaping portion of His gifts. Scripture gives us some startling examples of Solomon's gift of wisdom and his unusual wealth.

For the story of two mothers who needed Solomon's wisdom read **I Kings 3:16-28.**

16 Then two prostitutes came to the king and stood before him. 17 The one woman said, "Oh, my lord, this woman and I live in the same house, and I gave birth to a child while she was in the house. 18 Then on the third day after I gave birth, this woman also gave birth. And we were alone. There was no one else with us in the house; only we two were in the house. 19 And this woman's son died in the night, because she lay on him. 20 And she arose at midnight and took my son from beside me, while your servant slept, and laid him at her breast, and laid her dead son at my breast. 21 When I rose in the morning to nurse my child, behold, he was dead. But when I looked at him closely in the morning, behold, he was not the child that I had borne." 22 But the other woman said, "No, the living child is mine, and the dead child is yours." The first said, "No, the dead child is yours, and the living child is mine." Thus they spoke before the king.

23 Then the king said, "The one says, 'This is my son that is alive, and your son is dead'; and the other says, 'No; but your son is dead, and my son is the living one.'" 24 And the king said, "Bring me a sword." So a sword was brought before the king. 25 And the king said, "Divide the living child in two, and give half to the one and half to the other." 26 Then the woman whose son was alive said to the king, because her heart yearned for her son, "Oh, my lord, give her the living child, and by no means put him to death." But the other said, "He shall be neither mine nor yours; divide him." 27 Then the king answered and said, "Give the living child to the first woman, and by no means put him to death; she is his mother." 28 And all Israel heard of the judgment that the king had rendered, and they stood in awe of the king, because they perceived that the wisdom of God was in him to do justice.

According to this story, how did Solomon demonstrate God's gift of supernatural wisdom after he prayed for it?

Read II Chronicles 9:1-8 to see how the Queen of Sheba was affected by Solomon's wisdom.

¹Now when the queen of Sheba heard of the fame of Solomon, she came to Jerusalem to test him with hard questions, having a very great retinue and camels bearing spices and very much gold and precious stones. And when she came to Solomon, she told him all that was on her mind. ²And Solomon answered all her questions. There was nothing hidden from Solomon that he could not explain to her. ³And when the queen of Sheba had seen the wisdom of Solomon, the house that he had built, ⁴the food of his table, the seating of his officials, and the attendance of his servants, and their clothing, his cupbearers, and their clothing, and his burnt offerings that he offered at the house of the LORD, there was no more breath in her.

⁵And she said to the king, "The report was true that I heard in my own land of your words and of your wisdom, ⁶but I did not believe the reports until I came and my own eyes had seen it. And behold, half the greatness of your wisdom was not told me; you surpass the report that I heard. ⁷Happy are your wives! Happy are these your servants, who continually stand before you and hear your wisdom! ⁸Blessed be the LORD your God, who has delighted in you and set you on his throne as king for the LORD your God! Because your God loved Israel and would establish them forever, he has made you king over them, that you may execute justice and righteousness."

What did the Queen of Sheba recognize about Solomon's unusual wisdom?

Read I Kings 4:29-34.
²⁹And God gave Solomon wisdom and understanding beyond measure, and breadth of mind like the sand on the seashore, ³⁰so that Solomon's wisdom surpassed the wisdom of all the people of the east and all the wisdom of Egypt. ³¹For he was wiser than all other men, wiser than Ethan the Ezrahite, and Heman, Calcol, and Darda, the sons of Mahol, and his fame was in all the surrounding nations. ³²He also spoke 3,000 proverbs, and his songs were 1,005. ³³He spoke of trees, from the cedar that is in Lebanon to the hyssop that grows out of the wall. He spoke also of beasts, and of birds, and of reptiles, and of fish. ³⁴And people of all nations came to hear the wisdom of Solomon, and from all the kings of the earth, who had heard of his wisdom.

Describe Solomon's mind.

Who were the four wise men, besides Solomon, who are listed in this passage?

Which chapter of the Bible was written by Ethan the Ezrahite, one of the wise men to whom Solomon was compared? (Google his name.)

Read I Chronicles 6:31-33.
³¹These are the men whom David put in charge of the service of song in the house of the Lord after the ark rested there. ³²They ministered with song before the tabernacle of the tent of meeting until Solomon built the house of the Lord in Jerusalem, and they performed their service according to their order. ³³These are the men who served and their sons. Of the sons of the Kohathites: Heman the singer the son of Joel, son of Samuel.

What was Heman's role in both David and Solomon's courts?

Which chapter of the Bible was written by Heman, one of the wise men to whom Solomon was compared? (Google "Heman in the Bible.")

The Bible says Solomon's wisdom surpassed the wisdom of both the people of the East and of Egypt, and that was saying a lot. The ancient Near East produced a lot of "wisdom literature"—texts that instruct the reader about life, virtue and social interaction. The wise men of that region in ancient times wrote instructive as well as reflective texts. Ecclesiastes has both. Some scholars would classify Proverbs as the workbook for a beginning, or "undergraduate course" in wisdom, while Ecclesiastes is the advanced or "graduate school" text.[3]

We find an example in the writings of two Egyptian wise men in 1100 BC, 100 years before Solomon. *The Instructions of Amenemope* and *The Instructions of 'Onchsheshonqy* were two examples of wisdom literature brilliantly written by men who were considered some of the wisest Egypt ever produced. They wrote proverbs and maxims for Egyptians that were read worldwide. But Solomon's wisdom far exceeded their own.[4]

In today's world, how would we write I Kings 4:31?
"For he was wiser than all other men, wiser than

Born in Boston in 1898, William James Sidis made the headlines in the early twentieth century as a child prodigy with an amazing intellect. To put his intellect in perspective, Albert Einstein's IQ is estimated at 160, Leonardo da Vinci's at 180 and Isaac Newton's at 190. Sidis is thought to have had an IQ between 275-300. He could read the New York Times before he was 2. At age 6, his language repertoire included English, Latin, French, German, Russian, Hebrew, Turkish and Armenian. At age 11, he entered Harvard University as one of the youngest students in the school's history.[5]

But Sidis was no match for Solomon, whose wisdom was far greater.

In which intellectual disciplines was Solomon an expert?

Can you just imagine how smart Solomon was? After God answered his request for an understanding heart to rule the people, He then added all types of wisdom and knowledge, and Solomon's mind must have raced with the heightened electricity flowing through his brain. Knowledge of many subjects came pouring into His mind from the mind of God. He understood arts and sciences, history, mathematics and music. He was an expert in biology and botany, zoology and philosophy, psychology, theology and was a gifted song-writer. He had unusual discernment in criminal justice and legal matters. In our day, he would have had multiple doctorates in several disciplines of science, psychology, music, and languages. He would have made Sir Isaac Newton, Albert Einstein, Ludwig Beethoven, Wolfgang Mozart, Stephen Hawking and Bill Gates look simple-minded and small.

What decision are you facing now that needs the wisdom of Solomon?

More than just knowledge, Solomon had the wisdom to know how to apply it. "In literary history and beyond, wisdom is generally understood as a mental quality most common in older people, and familiarity with a set of customs and practices acquired through long experience rather than book learning or spontaneous revelation. You can learn calculus, physics, violin, sculpture, or gymnastics as a child. But only through years of experience – through ups and downs that trace lines around your eyes – can you acquire wisdom."[6]

Read Proverbs 2:1-15.

¹*My son, if you receive my words and treasure up my commandments with you, ²making your ear attentive to wisdom and inclining your heart to understanding; ³yes, if you call out for insight and raise your voice for understanding, ⁴if you seek it like silver and search for it as for hidden treasures, ⁵then you will understand the fear of the LORD and find the knowledge of God. ⁶For the LORD gives wisdom; from his mouth come knowledge and understanding; ⁷he stores up sound wisdom for the upright; he is a shield to those who walk in integrity, ⁸guarding the paths of justice and watching over the way of his saints.*

⁹*Then you will understand righteousness and justice and equity, every good path; ¹⁰for wisdom will come into your heart, and knowledge will be pleasant to your soul; ¹¹discretion will watch over you, understanding will guard you, ¹²delivering you from the way of evil, from men of perverted speech, ¹³who forsake the paths of uprightness to walk in the ways of darkness, ¹⁴who rejoice in doing evil and delight in the perverseness of evil, ¹⁵men whose paths are crooked, and who are devious in their ways.*

List the things the Lord gives to us, according to verses 6-8?

You might end your time of study with the following prayer: *"Lord, give me wisdom and discernment to make important decisions according to Your will. Show me the right path and open and close doors before me. I trust You, and I will follow You. I ask this in the name of Jesus. Amen."*

[3]*Archaeological Study Bible, NIV, An Illustrated Walk through Biblical History and Culture,* Zondervan, 2005, p 960.
[4]*The Literature of Ancient Egypt,* edited by William Kelly Simpson and published by Yale University Press.
[5] "Meet William James Sidis: The Smartest Guy Ever?" npr.com.
[6] "The Pros and Cons of Wisdom," Episode 6, literatureandhistory.com.

A Bit of Wisdom

What big decisions do you need to make in the next month?

In the next 3 months?

Next year?

Try this: Begin reading a chapter in Psalms and one in Proverbs, and record verses that speak to your questions. Keep reading and praying through Psalms and Proverbs until God speaks to you in a way you can hear and understand what He wants you to do. Ask Him to give you wisdom according to His will.

Money, Money, Money — Day 4

Heavenly Father, thank You for Your many, abundant blessings given to me and my family. Thank You for supplying our needs. Now, Lord, show us how to be a blessing to others, passing on Your blessings where they are needed. I love You, Lord. In Jesus' name. Amen.

CELINA needed help. She and Paul just couldn't seem to stop spending money. They didn't buy "bad" things, but it seemed all those little online expenditures added up to more than they had each month. And the house and car always seemed to need repairs. The credit card bills never got fully paid. They just needed a little more money–or a lot more. Then their problems would be solved. They could relax and get out from under this stress. They were getting too old for this! She knew there had to be a way out. They needed to talk to someone really wise with solid answers for straightening out this mess and to hear from someone who had lots of money and knew how to manage it well. Her sisters had told her they were studying Ecclesiastes. She wondered if Solomon could help them as well?

Read II Chronicles 1:12.

"...I will also give you riches, possessions, and honor, such as none of the kings had who were before you, and none after you shall have the like."

What three things did God give Solomon in addition to wisdom and understanding?

Read II Chronicles 9:13-16 to discover the enormity of Solomon's wealth.

¹³Now the weight of gold that came to Solomon in one year was 666 talents of gold, ¹⁴besides that which the explorers and merchants brought. And all the kings of Arabia and the governors of the land brought gold and silver to Solomon. ¹⁵King Solomon made 200 large shields of beaten gold; 600 shekels of beaten gold went into each shield. ¹⁶And he made 300 shields of beaten gold; 300 shekels of gold went into each shield; and the king put them in the House of the Forest of Lebanon.

Do a Google search for the value of Solomon's income of 666 talents of gold. How much money is it in your currency?

What other revenue streams of income did he receive regularly?

What did Solomon do with some of his gold according to verses 15 and 16?

What do you think those shields represented for him?

Solomon had an income of a modern-day equivalent of approximately 1 billion US dollars per year. His wealth was staggering. He could have anything, buy anything, build anything, own anything or anyone. His wealth was greater than Amazon founder Jeff Bezos, the richest man in the world, according to the Forbes billionaires' list.

He could have all of the finest palaces fitted out with the most extravagant furnishings. He could eat the most exquisite foods and wear the most expensive clothes. He had servants, slaves, wives and concubines to fulfill his every desire. There was nothing he had to wait for and nothing on his wish list. He could have everything right now.

Read II Chronicles 9:17-19.

17 The king also made a great ivory throne and overlaid it with pure gold. 18 The throne had six steps and a footstool of gold, which were attached to the throne, and on each side of the seat were armrests and two lions standing beside the armrests, 19 while twelve lions stood there, one on each end of a step on the six steps. Nothing like it was ever made for any kingdom.

Describe Solomon's throne:

Read II Chronicles 9:20-22.

20 All King Solomon's drinking vessels were of gold, and all the vessels of the House of the Forest of Lebanon were of pure gold. Silver was not considered as anything in the days of Solomon. 21 For the king's ships went to Tarshish with the servants of Hiram. Once every three years the ships of Tarshish used to come bringing gold, silver, ivory, apes, and peacocks. 22 Thus King Solomon excelled all the kings of the earth in riches and in wisdom.

According to these verses, how did Solomon and his guests eat and drink in his palace?

What was the name of one of his palaces in his royal complex and why do you think this was its name?

What did Solomon import from Tarshish every three years?

Fill in the blanks from II Chronicles 9:22:

Thus King Solomon _____ all the kings of the earth _____ and _____ .

Read II Chronicles 9:23-28.

²³And all the kings of the earth sought the presence of Solomon to hear his wisdom, which God had put into his mind. ²⁴Every one of them brought his present, articles of silver and of gold, garments, myrrh, spices, horses, and mules, so much year by year. ²⁵And Solomon had 4,000 stalls for horses and chariots, and 12,000 horsemen, whom he stationed in the chariot cities and with the king in Jerusalem. ²⁶And he ruled over all the kings from the Euphrates to the land of the Philistines and to the border of Egypt. ²⁷And the king made silver as common in Jerusalem as stone, and he made cedar as plentiful as the sycamore of the Shephelah. ²⁸And horses were imported for Solomon from Egypt and from all lands.

Why did the kings of the earth come to Solomon?

What did each one of them bring to Solomon that further increased his wealth?

✺ What did God give to Solomon besides wisdom?

✺ How much money did Solomon have and why did he have it?

What item was on earth in Solomon's time that he couldn't buy?

Solomon was wealthier than we can imagine. Besides the income from taxes, the kings in surrounding nations gladly came to pay tribute to him just to hear his astounding wisdom and knowledge. They brought gold, frankincense, and myrrh, just as the kings did to newborn Jesus almost 1000 years later. They heaped gifts upon Solomon and his kingdom. Solomon was blessed and gifted by God like no other.

A Bit of Wisdom

When you are under stress, one of the things that's hardest to manage is money. Compared to what you're going through, your finances seem inconsequential. But life on earth requires us to be good stewards. Bills must be paid, accounts reconciled, and taxes filed. If you can't handle that right now, find a trustworthy person who can help you. It might be for a short season or long term. Reach out and get help before your finances become yet another burden. The last thing you need is to be overwhelmed by a monetary crisis. Ask God to bring to you just the right person for the job.

PUFF OF SMOKE — Day 5

Lord Jesus, I thank You for who You are and all that You have done for me. Bless You for Your sacrifice for me that I might be in a relationship with You. Now, Lord, I bring You my questions and concerns, my problems and trials and lay them at Your feet. Take them and show me how to walk by faith, even when I cannot see the way ahead of me. I trust You, and I love You. In Jesus' name. Amen.

Stephen and Elizabeth loved to go river rafting. The thrill of the rapids, the adrenaline rush of near disasters, the quiet float down a majestic river, the wildlife on the river banks, and the exercise of paddling all added up to a perfect day for them. When the water level was high and the sun was shining, there was nothing like it.

But with first her diagnosis of lupus, then Stephen's death, Elizabeth was on a journey of the river of life that had brought a series of rapids and rocks. While her prayer life was strong and her knowledge of Scripture helped, she still found herself crying out, "Why?" Her faith was being tested to the core. She decided to join her sisters by diving into Ecclesiastes for answers. Right from the start, she could identify with Solomon. He begins his sermon with a bold cry.

Read Ecclesiastes 1:2, 3.
²Vanity of vanities, says the Preacher, ³What does man gain by all the toil at which he toils under the sun?

The New International Version says it this way: "Meaningless! Meaningless!" says the Teacher. "Utterly meaningless! Everything is meaningless."

Which word is repeated by Solomon over and over in this verse? Find it in several translations.

What does this word mean to you?

Where exactly is "under the sun?"

How would you answer the Preacher's question in verse 3?

How did Jesus expand on this question in Mark 8:36, 37?

³⁶ For what does it profit a man to gain the whole world and forfeit his soul?
³⁷ For what can a man give in return for his soul?

Solomon was intelligent and discerning and able to be objective about life on earth. He used one word to summarize it: Vanity! This word "vanity" means "breath" like a puff of smoke. There is no substance to it.

So, the wisest and wealthiest man who ever lived said this is the summary of all things? It's nothing? It's a puff of smoke that's here today and forever gone? Yikes! No wonder everyone says this book is a "downer." But wait! Did you catch the key phrase that goes with the key word? Over and over Solomon tells us that he is observing "life under the sun" when he describes it as meaningless. "Under the sun" means life here on earth that you can observe with your five senses. It is life on this planet with no consideration for God, faith, and the supernatural. That is the life that is meaningless.

The Preacher is going to repeatedly say, "vanity" and "under the sun." ("Vanity" is repeated 38 times and is the key word of the book.) By saying, "Vanity of vanities" he is using superlative language that means "breath of breaths." He exclaims that life is just a vapor. And he writes it in bold print and underlines it by saying, "ALL is vanity!" It is a powerful statement to open his sermon and command the attention of his audience. What if your pastor opened his sermon next Sunday with those words? I imagine everyone would perk up and listen!

Then, he gives his hearers the location of these vanities. They are "under the sun." This refers to life on *terra firma* that every person on earth experiences and observes. It is in contrast to what's in the heavenlies and the spiritual realm—God, Jesus, the Spirit, angels, and faith. His opening theme cries out to us that life down here is rough. It starts out hard and gets harder. When we only see life from earth's point of view, it's pretty bleak. Everything we thought would be reliable isn't, and everything that is supposed to satisfy us doesn't. The world is broken. But thankfully, if we keep listening to him, the Preacher will bring us into the light.

Read Ecclesiastes 1:4-7.

⁴A generation goes, and a generation comes, but the earth remains forever. ⁵The sun rises, and the sun goes down, and hastens to the place where it rises. ⁶The wind blows to the south and goes around to the north; around and around goes the wind, and on its circuits the wind returns. ⁷All streams run to the sea, but the sea is not full; to the place where the streams flow, there they flow again.

Do you think the Preacher is at the beginning of his adulthood, the midpoint, or the end of his adult life when we wrote these words?

How does he describe the cycle of life?

We are about to study this man's life and read the Last Will and Testament of King Solomon, the wisest, richest man who ever lived. He had unlimited resources, wealth, and unfathomable wisdom. This man who had it all, tried it all, tasted it all, experienced it all, is willing to show us the way down the river. If he were doing a lecture series, would you buy a ticket? Well, here it is, captured for you in the book of Ecclesiastes. This incredibly gifted man is in his Winter Season. He's coming to the end of his amazingly colorful life and looks back to impart his final analysis of life on earth: the good, the bad, and the ugly.

Read Ecclesiastes 1:8-11.
⁸All things are full of weariness; a man cannot utter it; the eye is not satisfied with seeing, nor the ear filled with hearing. ⁹What has been is what will be, and what has been done is what will be done, and there is nothing new under the sun. ¹⁰Is there a thing of which it is said, "See, this is new"? It has been already in the ages before us. ¹¹There is no remembrance of former things, nor will there be any remembrance of later things yet to be among those who come after.

Verse 9 contains a famous phrase that is often quoted. Write it here.

___

Why is the Preacher frustrated in these verses? What is he searching for but can't find?

An ancient Assyrian, Tatianus, showed the Grecians how all the arts they treasured were actually originated by their enemies. "For shame, do not call those things 'inventions' which are but 'imitations!' For surely there is nothing new under the sun."⁷

Solomon was bored. He searched the world over for something new to see, hear, and experience; but he couldn't find it. Have you ever said, "There's nothing new under the sun" when fashions that went "out" are suddenly back "in?" When colors that became ugly and outdated are now the rage? Our senses are bombarded with information, education, and entertainment, and after a while nothing looks or sounds new or good any more.

Sometimes we watch television or surf the internet looking for something we haven't already seen, only to find re-runs of news stories, movies and television programs. Even with hundreds of channels and several streaming devices, nothing is appealing. This must be how Solomon felt. He had seen everything available in his day, and he was bored to tears. This is the best life offers "under the sun."

Solomon summarized for us at the beginning of his sermon what life is like without reference to God. It comes up short. But we have the whole of God's Word to lay over Solomon's assessment of life. Yes, "under the sun", it is troublesome. But as believers in Jesus Christ, we have the New Testament, the new revelation of God's plan and purpose for His children on earth.

Read II Corinthians 5:17.
Therefore, if anyone is in Christ, he is a new creation. The old has passed away; behold, the new has come.

✹ What is truly new that Solomon didn't understand?

While on earth, the cycles of life, nature, and even our thoughts go on in endless cycles, but what IS new is a man or woman when they've been re-created as a new creature in Christ. The old life, old sins have passed away, and now life really is new.

Solomon had unlimited resources, supernatural wisdom, expansive power, and sexual fulfillment; and he begins his sermon with an outburst. I hear him saying, "It's all a puff of smoke! It's all vanity! It doesn't satisfy like I thought it would. I'm bored, looking for something new."

Stop for a moment and think about how God has made you a new creation. If you have prayed, "Lord, I surrender my life to You. Please forgive me of my sins; please take control of my life," Your old nature that loved to sin has been dealt with on the Cross of Jesus. You now have a new nature and the mind of Christ. YOU are something new on the earth. You are a human being, living, breathing and walking on this earth carrying around a precious treasure—the life of Jesus. Jesus, who loved you so much He sacrificed His life; Jesus, who spoke truth in love; Jesus, who loved His enemies; Jesus, who believed God could feed 5,000 people from five loaves and two fish. HIS life is in you if you have given over your life to Him personally.

Our world IS broken. Things rotate in endless cycles of generations that come and go. That is true of life "under the sun." But for those of us who know Jesus Christ as Lord of our lives, that is not the whole story! If we have bowed our knees before Him and surrendered our lives into His hands, God's faithfulness is new every morning! Our past is gone, and we are new creatures who have gone from death to life. We live "above the sun" with the Son of God in a real, vibrant, moment-by-moment relationship—a relationship that satisfies our heart and fills our longings. And He leads us into a life full of purpose and meaning. Meaningless, Solomon? No, with Jesus, it is meaningful!

If you have never accepted Christ personally as Lord and Savior of your life and experienced the new life He gives, we invite you to do that now.
- Ask Him to forgive all your sins and receive His forgiveness.
- Believe in your heart that Jesus died to save you from the penalty of your sins.
- Confess that Jesus is Lord and Savior of your life and commit yourself into His hands to lead you for the rest of your life.

[7]"The Pros and Cons of Wisdom, Episode 6," historyandliterature.com.

A Bit of Wisdom

A good example of "nothing new under the sun" can be seen on our screens. Most movies today become franchises so they can take the same old story line, then just stretch and embellish it to become five or six films, increasing their revenue exponentially. Because of streaming services, we can watch old programs to our heart's content. But is that the best use of our time? You might be watching television with your phone in your hand, the TV blaring, while you scroll the iPad on your lap to see the Instagram postings of your friends. Does that sound like an overload for your brain? Researchers tell us, yes, probably.

So how about calling a media fast…even if it's just for a few hours a day. Let's take a brain break. Light a candle and sit quietly for a while, then put on instrumental praise music. Let peace steal over you. Breathe and let your mind and heart reset.

BIBLE STUDY NOTES

WEEK 2
WHAT IS THE BEST WAY TO LIVE MY LIFE?

A Personal Message to You from Solomon

You're going to want to satisfy the itch of chasing after achievements and possessions and filling the ache of loneliness. We were designed with a void, and your temptation will be to fill it with all kinds of things available to you. I've been there and have a lot to share with you about what can really satisfy your heart. I hope you'll listen to me better than I listened to both my heavenly and earthly fathers. If you will listen, you'll be on the right road and will have a meaningful life.

Smart or Wise? — Day 1

Lord Jesus, I long to know the truth that will set me free in this season and to have meaning and purpose in my life. Show me the way. Lead me with Your wisdom, Your mind and Your heart. I love You and trust You, Jesus. It is in Your matchless name I pray. Amen.

Luke, Madeline's missionary husband, was pressing in to finalize his dissertation. His doctorate was within reach, but it was going to require long days, short nights and time away from the family to get it done. He hated to admit it, but the initials "PhD" after his name meant a lot to him. He couldn't wait to be Dr. Bisset. After all, being an expert in the field of international family relations would apply to the new missions assignment he was considering, but he knew he was missing out on some important things going on in his own family. Madeline was trying to make up for his absences, but it was causing a strain. What should he do?

Read Ecclesiastes 1:12-18.
[12]I the Preacher have been king over Israel in Jerusalem. [13]And I applied my heart to seek and to search out by wisdom all that is done under heaven. It is an unhappy business that God has given to the children of man to be busy with. [14]I have seen everything that is done under the sun, and behold, all is vanity and a striving after wind. [15]What is crooked cannot be made straight, and what is lacking cannot be counted. [16]I said in my heart, "I have acquired great wisdom, surpassing all who were over Jerusalem before me, and my heart has had great experience of wisdom and knowledge." [17]And I applied my heart to know wisdom and to know madness and folly. I perceived that this also is but a striving after wind. [18]For in much wisdom is much vexation, and he who increases knowledge increases sorrow.

What is Solomon searching for in verses 13 and 17?

What is his conclusion in both verses?

In the last part of verse 17, Solomon summarizes his conclusion about only increasing knowledge instead of wisdom. Write his conclusion here in your own words.

_____

_____

Solomon's great wealth enabled him to make his court the center of learning for Israel and the surrounding nations. He pursued the highest level of intellectual pursuit with his genius mind. Like-minded scholars must have loved the court of Solomon where they could discuss the great issues of the day and sharpen one another's insights. His was the think-tank of his day.

Solomon looks back down the road of life at us and shouts back, "Fulfillment isn't here! If you think being smart, achieving the highest ranks, making it to the top in your field will satisfy the ache in your heart, think again. When you get to the top, you're going to say to yourself, 'Is that all there is?' You'll never be smarter than me, no matter how much you study. You'll never achieve more than me, so don't go there. I went to the top in every field available in my generation. No one exceeded me; I was number one. And I can tell you, this is not where to find meaning and worth. Your IQ scores, doctoral degrees, and fancy letters behind your name won't matter much to you when you are older. Your job title, your résumé and your profile on social media are only outward appearances. If you pursue that and nothing else, you'll end up at the top of the ladder of worldly success but just a shell of a person with nothing to show for your life but a certificate—a piece of paper—and you won't care. What your heart longs for is true identify, true faith, true hope, and true love. And you'll find all that and more in God."

Week 2: Day 1

Solomon wanted to solve the mysteries of the universe on his own. He wanted to be able to use his amazing mind to understand everything about everything. But the human brain isn't capable of that. Solomon came to a shocking conclusion. The more he learned and the wiser he became, the more he realized what he didn't know. It made him frustrated and sad that, no matter how much he pursued wisdom and knowledge, they were always out of reach, moving just ahead of him. My mother used to say, "The more you know, the more you realize you don't know a thing!" She was an avid reader, a hungry student of wisdom and truth in the Word of God up into her 90's. And this was her conclusion: "We're all just kindergarteners!"

Doctors, lawyers, scientists, seminarians, theologians, and all others pursuing the truth at high levels are doing a good thing to expand their intellect and gain wisdom. But the wisest among them realize that on earth, we must temper our enthusiasm for intellectual pursuits alone. Yes, of course, we should study, but we would do well to understand that intellectual achievement is not the end-goal and won't buy us ultimate wisdom. True wisdom comes from God alone.

Paul knew the source of wisdom and describes it in **I Corinthians 1:26-29:**

^{26}Brothers and sisters, think of what you were when you were called. Not many of you were wise by human standards; not many were influential; not many were of noble birth. ^{27}But God chose the foolish things of the world to shame the wise; God chose the weak things of the world to shame the strong. ^{28}God chose the lowly things of this world and the despised things—and the things that are not—to nullify the things that are, ^{29}so that no one may boast before him. ^{30}It is because of him that you are in Christ Jesus, who has become for us wisdom from God—that is, our righteousness, holiness and redemption. ^{31}Therefore, as it is written: "Let the one who boasts boast in the Lord.

Where do we obtain true wisdom according to verse 30?

How does Paul describe wisdom from God?

None of us can boast in our wisdom; not even Solomon. No matter how wise you are, God is always wiser. Our true wisdom comes from Jesus Christ who "has become for us wisdom from God." Jesus IS our wisdom. Solomon began well in his spring season by walking with God in the light of His wisdom, but his heart was darkened by disobedience and sin. It nearly drove him mad.

Read Ecclesiastes 2:12-17.

¹²So I turned to consider wisdom and madness and folly. For what can the man do who comes after the king? Only what has already been done. ¹³Then I saw that there is more gain in wisdom than in folly, as there is more gain in light than in darkness. ¹⁴The wise person has his eyes in his head, but the fool walks in darkness. And yet I perceived that the same event happens to all of them. ¹⁵Then I said in my heart, "What happens to the fool will happen to me also. Why then have I been so very wise?" And I said in my heart that this also is vanity. ¹⁶For of the wise as of the fool there is no enduring remembrance, seeing that in the days to come all will have been long forgotten. How the wise dies just like the fool! ¹⁷So I hated life, because what is done under the sun was grievous to me, for all is vanity and a striving after wind.

What two things does Solomon contrast in verse 12?

To what does he compare wisdom and folly?

In verse 16, he realizes something that makes him hate life. What is it?

We are reading Solomon's wise words even today. He thought they would be long forgotten, but he was wrong. God preserved for us the wisdom He gave Solomon, and his words have lived through the centuries after him. When we are faithful to the assignment God gives to us, we don't need to fret about what happens to that work after we are gone. It's all up to Him.

Week 2: Day 1

Look at the difference in the tone of the passage above and the one Solomon wrote in **Proverbs 2:6-12**.

⁶For the LORD gives wisdom; from his mouth come knowledge and understanding; ⁷he stores up sound wisdom for the upright; he is a shield to those who walk in integrity, ⁸guarding the paths of justice and watching over the way of his saints. ⁹Then you will understand righteousness and justice and equity, every good path; ¹⁰ for wisdom will come into your heart, and knowledge will be pleasant to your soul; ¹¹discretion will watch over you, understanding will guard you, ¹²delivering you from the way of evil, from men of perverted speech.

✹ What did Solomon already know about finding wisdom?

✹ What did he say about wisdom, knowledge, discretion and understanding in verse 10?

✹ Why do you think he lost his way?

In Ecclesiastes, Solomon looked from a secular point of view; and the viewpoint was bleak. He saw that both the fool and the wise man die in the end and he thought no one even remembered what they did. He asked the question, "What is the point?" We see this kind of desperation and despair in so many people today who long for answers to life's perplexities but are looking in all the wrong places. Earlier in his life, Solomon knew where to find the answers. He knew all true wisdom stems from God alone.

James directs our search in the right direction. Read **James 1:5** and fill in the blanks:

If any of you lacks _____, you should _____ God, who gives _____ to all without finding fault, and it will be given to you.

Paul, a brilliant man with an attorney's mind had this to say about wisdom:
I Corinthians 2:1-16.

¹And I, when I came to you, brothers, did not come proclaiming to you the testimony of God with lofty speech or wisdom. ²For I decided to know nothing among you except Jesus Christ and him crucified. ³And I was with you in weakness and in fear and much trembling, ⁴and my speech and my message were not in plausible words of wisdom, but in demonstration of the Spirit and of power, ⁵so that your faith might not rest in the wisdom of men but in the power of God. ⁶Yet among the mature we do impart wisdom, although it is not a wisdom of this age or of the rulers of this age, who are doomed to pass away. ⁷But we impart a secret and hidden wisdom of God, which God decreed before the ages for our glory. ⁸None of the rulers of this age understood this, for if they had, they would not have crucified the Lord of glory. ⁹But, as it is written, "no eye has seen, nor ear heard, nor the heart of man imagined, what God has prepared for those who love him"—

¹⁰these things God has revealed to us through the Spirit. For the Spirit searches everything, even the depths of God. ¹¹For who knows a person's thoughts except the spirit of that person, which is in him? So also no one comprehends the thoughts of God except the Spirit of God. ¹²Now we have received not the spirit of the world, but the Spirit who is from God, that we might understand the things freely given us by God. ¹³And we impart this in words not taught by human wisdom but taught by the Spirit, interpreting spiritual truths to those who are spiritual. ¹⁴The natural person does not accept the things of the Spirit of God, for they are folly to him, and he is not able to understand them because they are spiritually discerned. ¹⁵The spiritual person judges all things, but is himself to be judged by no one. ¹⁶"For who has understood the mind of the Lord so as to instruct him?" But we have the mind of Christ.

According to verse 5, our faith should not rest in _____

but in _____.

While he's looking at life backward and upside down from "under the sun," Solomon shows us that the view from the bottom of life without God will never give you real wisdom and it will make you wonder if life is worth living. The view from the top, with God as our focus, living life in Christ, is a completely different viewpoint. It's the difference between *information* and *revelation*. We will understand the "secret and hidden wisdom of God" when the Spirit reveals it to us. He is more than willing to give us the secret of His wisdom if we will only ask.

WEEK 2: DAY 1

A Bit of Wisdom

Often, one of the issues of senior adulthood is having the wisdom to make decisions about your aging, ailing parents. Many first-world adult children move away from their hometown, so caring remotely for elderly parents becomes a stressful, heart-wrenching, time-consuming, financially impactful, emotional time bomb. And if you live in town, it's sometimes even harder. You are always "on call." Often, the acute needs of your parents have a sudden onset, and you must drop everything and run to their side. Or that's what you should do. Adult children and their siblings may be working together for the first time to make caregiving and financial decisions as a team. There is nothing easy about this season of life.

You need some wise counsel and guiding principles to employ. The first is "no regrets." When your parents are gone, you will want to say to yourself, "I don't want any regrets when this season is over. I want to do what I can now for my parents while they are still here. When they're gone, I want the satisfaction that I did all I could to be there, to bless and honor them, and to love my siblings through this process."

Wisdom Continued

The second principle is "self-care." My parents lived a four-hour drive from me while I was involved in supporting my sisters in their care. During the four years I was traveling back and forth, I didn't do a good job of self-care. I gained a lot of weight and rarely exercised. I was stressed and grieving, even while my parents were still with us. If I had it to do over again, I would focus on loving myself as I loved them. Elder care isn't a sprint; it's a marathon. I needed to pace myself, take care of my own health, and give myself space to process my feelings of loss and grief. After they were gone, I spent months caring for my body that was in sad shape and allowing my bruised heart to heal. The pandemic of 2020 was actually a huge blessing for me in that regard. It was a forced retreat that was used by God in my life to heal my body, mind, and spirit.

The third principle in elder care is "let go." When dispersing your parent's earthly goods, there will be moments of anguish over dividing precious things with your siblings and even for the things that become yours, deciding how to make use of them. If you and your siblings are fighting over something valuable, why not share it by letting it stay in one house for five years and then moving to the next? And then there will be some things that you'll need to have a little ceremony to take pictures with it, cherish it and kiss it goodbye. At all costs, be a peacemaker and "let go." Nothing is worth damaging relationships.

TRUE HAPPINESS — Day 2

Lord Jesus, I choose to pursue You. Keep my heart focused. Don't let any distractions keep me from You: my phone, the internet, and constant messages bombarding me. Lord, thank You for technology and entertainment and pleasurable things to enjoy life but help me keep my priorities straight turning off those things that compete with my time with You. You are my first love, and there is no one like You.

CELINA AND PAUL knew it wasn't in the budget and would cost a fortune, but they got out the credit cards once again. The cost to go on a nice vacation was staggering and Celina knew they'd be paying for months and maybe years to come…with compounded interest. They'd never pay off those bills. Was it worth it? Maybe not, but they just wanted to get away! They needed a break and to spend that break somewhere nice. They closed their eyes to the consequences and took the plunge.

Read Ecclesiastes 2:1-11.

¹I said in my heart, "Come now, I will test you with pleasure; enjoy yourself." But behold, this also was vanity. ²I said of laughter, "It is mad," and of pleasure, "What use is it?" ³I searched with my heart how to cheer my body with wine—my heart still guiding me with wisdom—and how to lay hold on folly, till I might see what was good for the children of man to do under heaven during the few days of their life. ⁴I made great works. I built houses and planted vineyards for myself. ⁵I made myself gardens and parks, and planted in them all kinds of fruit trees. ⁶I made myself pools from which to water the forest of growing trees. ⁷I bought male and female slaves, and had slaves who were born in my house. I had also great possessions of herds and flocks, more than any who had been before me in Jerusalem. ⁸I also gathered for myself silver and gold and the treasure of kings and provinces. I got singers, both men and women, and many concubines, the delight of the sons of man.

⁹So I became great and surpassed all who were before me in Jerusalem. Also, my wisdom remained with me. ¹⁰And whatever my eyes desired I did not keep from them. I kept my heart from no pleasure, for my heart found pleasure in all my toil, and this was my reward for all my toil. ¹¹Then I considered all that my hands had done and the toil I had expended in doing it, and behold, all was vanity and a striving after wind, and there was nothing to be gained under the sun.

Solomon decides if wisdom isn't the answer, he'd try something else to find meaning and purpose in life. What did he try?

✹ List the projects he engaged in to bring pleasure to himself.

✹ What is his final assesment of all of these pleasurable projects stated in verse 11?

The more he is entertained, the more he wants entertainment, only to realize he's seen it all before. The more women he adds to his harem, the more they must have made him realize his need for one true love. His new building projects lost their newness so quickly. Everything he thinks will satisfy his thirst for something exciting and new turns out to be an imitation of something already discovered, already experienced, already documented. He tried women, wine, and song, he tried extravagant food and was the architect of amazing buildings, and he had more money than he knew what to do with. And all he had to say when looking back on his life was, "So what?"

One of the best things about retirement is having the time to do things you've always wanted to do. Go on a cruise, live on the lake, take that long-awaited trip, have fun with friends, and more. If you can afford those things, of course, they're great to enjoy. God created pleasurable things to delight us.

But David and I know of couples who literally spend all of their retirement on a cruise ship, taking 20-30 cruises a year. (At least they did pre-COVID-19.) They are cruising through life during their "golden years." They are eating and gambling their best remaining years away. Is that all there is to life?

While author Margaret Nash (*Rebellious Aging and Retirement Rebel*) and I have few lifestyle choices in common, I appreciate her assessment of what it's like to be retired and plunged into the Winter Season. Winter Season people who are retired don't have to work, don't have the responsibility for children full time, don't have deadlines and don't have to do things they don't want to do. For younger people that sounds like heaven. But there are also challenges with first-world retirement. There are too many CHANGES at once—having an empty nest, relocating at the same time as retirement, lacking structure in their schedule, caring for elderly parents, and feeling overwhelmed about it all. There are also too many CHOICES—causing the feeling of being stuck, lacking motivation and ambition, missing structured aspects of your old life, and experiencing restlessness. There is too much CLUTTER—hanging on to things from the past that don't have relevance now or for future generations. And finally, too little CHALLENGE—despite the time and money to do what you wish, being plagued by boredom with too much time to watch TV, surf the internet, and look at your phone. While many people dream of retirement, when you have too much free time, money and comfort, it actually might not make you happy.[1]

Solomon warns us in verse 11 that pursuing pleasure as an end to itself is vanity, and striving after the wind brings nothing to be gained. There is so very much more to life!

Read John 10:9, 10.
⁹I am the door. If anyone enters by me, he will be saved and will go in and out and find pasture. ¹⁰The thief comes only to kill and steal and destroy. I came that they might have life and have it abundantly.

What does Jesus offer us instead of the pleasure Solomon was seeking?

What word pictures tell you how to find it?

Solomon has tried everything to find pleasure—and I mean everything. He tells us that it still didn't satisfy him. Jesus leads us to true pleasure in life. He's the door to open the way for us, and He's the Shepherd to lead us to abundant life.

Read I Timothy 6:17-19.
¹⁷As for the rich in this present age, charge them not to be haughty, nor to set their hopes on the uncertainty of riches, but on God, who richly provides us with everything to enjoy. ¹⁸They are to do good, to be rich in good works, to be generous and ready to share, ¹⁹thus storing up treasure for themselves as a good foundation for the future, so that they may take hold of that which is truly life.

✺ Complete this phrase from verse 17, "God, who richly provides us with_____

✺ What does that phrase mean to you?

What are the things we should do to make a deposit for the future?

When you let God direct your fun, your pleasure, He'll lead you to more joy-filled, fun opportunities than you ever dreamed. Just ask Him to direct your leisure time and then listen and follow His voice.

[1] *The Retirement Rebel: How To Get Your Life To Work, When You Don't Have To*, Margaret Nash, amazon.com

A Bit of Wisdom

Burn the candles!

While cleaning out my parents' house, we found dozens and dozens of candles. They were all colors and sizes of fragrant, beautiful candles with one thing in common. Not one had been lit—even once. They were probably 20 to 30 years old, and the day never came when my mama decided, "Today's the day to ENJOY my candles! I'm going to burn them, smell them, delight in them all the way until they're a puddle of wax." Being from the Great Generation that went through the Depression in the United States during the 1930's, she was taught to save, save, save and NEVER spend. She just couldn't give herself permission to fully enjoy her beautiful things. After my sisters and I divided all the candles, I took mine home and started burning one every day. For months, I enjoyed my mama's candles. When they were gone, I threw away the burned jars and the stubs and smiled. Those candles were finally enjoyed, Mama!

Passing the Baton — Day 3

Lord Jesus, I thank You for the work You have assigned to me. Thank You for the gifts and abilities You gave me to bring salt and light into the world, to improve the lot of others, and to share Your gifts. I also understand that there will come a day when it's time to allow others to step in and take the reins of this work. A time for me to step back and cheer on the next generation. Please give me the wisdom and grace to know that day when it comes, not to resist or deny it, but to embrace the change. I know I cannot do this without You. In my own weakness, I'll want to hold on too long, maintaining my position until long after the time I should let go. Help me, Lord. Speak to me. Give me the courage to follow You even in this. For it is in Your matchless name I pray. Amen.

Elizabeth had been teaching ESL (English as a Second Language) classes at church for 25 years. She'd seen lives changed as her students not only learned English skills but came to know Jesus personally. Apart from her family, it was one of the most fulfilling occupations of her life. But after Stephen died and with the progression of her disease, she knew it was time to pass the baton. However, it was so much harder than she'd imagined. She had poured her life into growing the ESL ministry from herself and two other volunteer teachers to a full-blown outreach of the church that was seeing more salvations and baptisms than any other part of their church family.

Besides the impact it made on whole families, it had made an impact on her. It gave her confidence, networked her with people all over the church and community, and filled a void. She loved it and didn't really want to give it up. Knowing it was time didn't make it any easier. So, Elizabeth began to pray. Praying was her "thing," so she got out her Bible and started studying every Scripture she could find about "legacy" and "mentoring." The results of her prayerful study led her in an interesting direction.

Read Ecclesiastes 2:18-23.

¹⁸I hated all my toil in which I toil under the sun, seeing that I must leave it to the man who will come after me, ¹⁹and who knows whether he will be wise or a fool? Yet he will be master of all for which I toiled and used my wisdom under the sun. This also is vanity. ²⁰So I turned about and gave my heart up to despair over all the toil of my labors under the sun, ²¹because sometimes a person who has toiled with wisdom and knowledge and skill must leave everything to be enjoyed by someone who did not toil for it. This also is vanity and a great evil. ²²What has a man from all the toil and striving of heart with which he toils beneath the sun? ²³For all his days are full of sorrow, and his work is a vexation. Even in the night his heart does not rest. This also is vanity.

In verses 18 and 19, Solomon is anguished about

_____

Underline the word "vanity" and the phrase "under the sun" in the passage above. How many words did you underline?

List the words that express Solomon's emotions in the passage above.

In one word, how would you say Solomon felt about leaving his work to others?

Solomon was bitter as he realized that all his toil with wisdom, knowledge and skill on the building and engineering projects during his lifetime would someday be enjoyed by the next generation who didn't work for it and probably didn't deserve it. He fumed when he saw that all the hard work to build and engineer exquisite buildings, to build up the armed forces, to establish the kingdom rule over other nations would, with his death, be handed over to his sons and to others in his court. From what we know of his sons, I don't blame him for seeing the folly in it all.

But there is another way to approach passing on a legacy. Moses and Elijah are great role models.

Read Deuteronomy 34:8, 9.

⁸And the people of Israel wept for Moses in the plains of Moab thirty days. Then the days of weeping and mourning for Moses were ended. ⁹And Joshua the son of Nun was full of the spirit of wisdom, for Moses had laid his hands on him. So the people of Israel obeyed him and did as the Lord had commanded Moses.

How did Moses pass the baton to Joshua?

Why did Joshua possess this wisdom?

Read Joshua 1:1-7.

¹After the death of Moses the servant of the LORD, the LORD said to Joshua the son of Nun, Moses' assistant, ²"Moses my servant is dead. Now therefore arise, go over this Jordan, you and all this people, into the land that I am giving to them, to the people of Israel. ³Every place that the sole of your foot will tread upon I have given to you, just as I promised to Moses. ⁴From the wilderness and this Lebanon as far as the great river, the river Euphrates, all the land of the Hittites to the Great Sea toward the going down of the sun shall be your territory. ⁵No man shall be able to stand before you all the days of your life. Just as I was with Moses, so I will be with you. I will not leave you or forsake you. ⁶Be strong and courageous, for you shall cause this people to inherit the land that I swore to their fathers to give them. ⁷Only be strong and very courageous, being careful to do according to all the law that Moses my servant commanded you. Do not turn from it to the right hand or to the left, that you may have good success wherever you go.

In verse 5, God makes a promise to Joshua about his succession. What was that promise?

Week 2: Day 3

According to verse 7, how was Joshua to carry out his assignment?

Moses intentionally blessed Joshua as his successor and prepared him for the transition in leadership to be as smooth as possible. Joshua had everything he needed to take the reins from Moses and lead Israel in the next part of their historic journey.

Read 1 Kings 19:15-17 for another story of succession, this time from Elijah to Elisha.
¹⁵*And the Lord said to him [Elijah], "Go, return on your way to the wilderness of Damascus. And when you arrive, you shall anoint Hazael to be king over Syria. ¹⁶And Jehu the son of Nimshi you shall anoint to be king over Israel, and Elisha the son of Shaphat of Abel-meholah you shall anoint to be prophet in your place.*

How did God instruct Elijah to pass the baton?

Read I Kings 19:19-21.
¹⁹*So he departed from there and found Elisha the son of Shaphat, who was plowing with twelve yoke of oxen in front of him, and he was with the twelfth. Elijah passed by him and cast his cloak upon him. ²⁰And he left the oxen and ran after Elijah and said, "Let me kiss my father and my mother, and then I will follow you." And he said to him, "Go back again, for what have I done to you?" ²¹And he returned from following him and took the yoke of oxen and sacrificed them and boiled their flesh with the yokes of the oxen and gave it to the people, and they ate. Then he arose and went after Elijah and assisted him.*

✦ What is the most interesting part of this story for you?

Moses and Elijah had anointed and powerful ministries to serve the Lord. They were key men in history, chosen by God. But they didn't live or serve forever on earth. Their life work, their time of ministry came to a close. But before they left, they each chose a man to take their place. They blessed and prepared the new man to take the reins.

Each of us has an assigned season to live out our purpose and take our own place in history. When you wrap your brain around the idea of blessing and preparing your own successor, it can bring great joy as you step back and they step forward. How you leave service at church, at work, or in ministry is up to you. Will you leave it with joy, blessing the new generation of leaders, or will you hold on too long, making the transition painful and difficult for everyone? Realizing that your work or your ministry doesn't belong to you but to God is the first step. Release it now into His hands. Then, ask God to reveal His plan for when and to whom you should pass it along to others He has chosen. And keep your eyes open for the one He brings into the picture.

Using the wisdom and knowledge God has given us, we need to mentor our successors and others of those who are younger in age and spiritual maturity. If you do not already have your "Joshua" or "Elisha" to mentor, ask God to give you someone who is ready for the wisdom you can pass on. Open your eyes to younger people around you. Your family members, your neighbors, workmates, church friends, or people in your gym may be waiting for someone to counsel them. The world needs a shoulder to cry on, a wise word spoken at just the right time, a listening ear. You may be called upon to do just that for someone you haven't noticed before. Be watching for the opportunities God brings to you for giving away the gifts of seasoned wisdom and experiential knowledge.

But don't stop with mentoring. We need to be making disciples for Jesus Christ. Here are some key points on how discipling is different than mentoring:

A disciple-making relationship must be holistic. It's not limited to a slice of life or specific skill but rather seeks to make an impact on every aspect of life. It must be this way because who we are influences everything: our attitudes, thoughts, words, and actions.

The discipler puts himself forward as the model. He echoes what Paul said in 1 Corinthians 11:1, "Follow my example as I follow the example of Christ." He doesn't say, "Be who I used to be," or "Do what I used to do," but rather, "Be who I am. Do what I do." This requires the discipler to be mature enough to live a life worthy of reproduction and humble enough to share where he falls short.

Disciple-making is generational. One of the primary reasons Jesus wanted to help the disciples was so that they would "fish for men." Jesus' essential message is to follow Him, to become like Him, to trade in our purpose for His purpose, to exchange the temporal for the eternal. He helped them so they'd help others. Jesus was focused on *multiplication, not addition.*[1]

If your Winter Season is about hardship and illness, pray for God to give you wisdom and knowledge to know which way to go on your journey by bringing you a mentor. There is someone who needs to mentor just as much as you need mentoring. Pay attention to those around you who have been where you are and can give you the support you need.

If your Winter Season is retirement, find someone to take under your wing. If you ask God, He will bring a person into your life who needs your spiritual guidance and emotional support.

✺ Who can be your "Moses," mentoring you into a deeper relationship with Jesus?

Who can be your "Joshua," allowing you to walk beside them as they follow Christ?

[1]"Mentoring vs. Disciple-making: What's the Difference?" by Justin Gravitt, Navigators Blog, March 27, 2018.

A Bit of Wisdom

Write out the main points of what you want to leave as a legacy for your children and grandchildren in a special journal. Perhaps it would follow this pattern:

What I wish someone had told me early in life:

What I have started that I hope you will continue:

This is the blessing I want to say over your life:

Joy, Joy, Joy Down In My Heart

Day 4

Lord Jesus, show me how to really enjoy life and bring enjoyment to those around me. Lord, I offer my resources to You—my heart and mind, the knowledge I've gained over the years, my energy and strength, and the money You've entrusted to me. It all belongs to You. Show me how to use my resources for Your purposes. I love You, Lord. It is in Your precious name I pray. Amen.

DAPHNE had been studying Ecclesiastes diligently, verse by verse. She'd made the decision to rise from the ashes of her divorce and become all that she could be according to God's plan. What did God want her to focus on now? How could she find contentment without Richard in her life? She was over 60 years old and never expected to be alone at this stage of life when they should have been enjoying their golden years together. It was so hard not to feel bitter about all the work she had put into their marriage and building their family. But now, she was living by herself in the big house she and Richard had built together. She was hosting their children alone on the holidays. While she missed being married, she was determined to make the best of her life. She had been engulfed in sorrow for long enough. God was taking care of her. Instead of wallowing in despair, grief and regret, she was going to move forward.

More than anything, Daphne needed joy. She needed to lighten up and do something fun with people who knew how to really enjoy life. So, in her Quiet Time with the Lord that morning, she decided to be bold and ask Him for ways to have good, clean fun!

She was specific in her prayer request, "Lord, I am asking You to show me how to enjoy my life now. I need a ray of sunshine to pierce through the darkness I've been living in for a long time. So today, would You show me how to find joy in something? I want to make joy-filled plans for a joy-filled future. I don't even know where to start. I don't have a lot of money to work with, and I can't afford a fancy vacation or to move to an exotic location. Please show me how to have good, healthy, wonderful fun on my budget. Show me who to include and what we should do to share these events in just the right way with just the right people. In Jesus' name I pray, knowing that You love me and want more for me than I want for myself. Amen!"

She knew the Lord would lead her to find joy in ways that would bring restoration and wholeness. She still had hard days to face, but she was determined to find something, even if it was a tiny thing, to celebrate. She was going to use her home and her resources to create peace, fun and fellowship for others. In fact, she knew some widows and other single women she would invite into her home to do just that. Today's reading in Ecclesiastes was exactly what she needed to hear.

Read Ecclesiastes 2:24, 25.
²⁴There is nothing better for a person than that he should eat and drink and find enjoyment in his toil. This also, I saw, is from the hand of God ²⁵for apart from him who can eat or who can have enjoyment?

✺ What three enjoyable things are listed in these verses?

✺ Why should we enjoy our lives?

✺ What do you need to change in your life to enjoy it more?

God isn't a kill-joy! He is the one who created life on earth to be enjoyed. He set man in the Garden of Eden; he didn't place him in a rock quarry to hammer out a miserable existence. But Solomon discovered that pursuing pleasure without God at the center of your life leads to disillusionment and even depression. Guilty pleasure isn't pleasurable at all. Overspending, overeating, getting addicted to your phone, your television, your computer and the internet all make promises they can't keep and will leave you feeling worse than ever. God is full of joy and when you connect to Him, to His abundant life, you can have more fun than anyone!

Enjoyment in life is one of God's gifts to us. Solomon tells us to "eat, drink, and be merry!" For those of us who need to lighten up, this is what the doctor ordered. If you are a little deficient in the "fun" category, take some pointers from your family. They can probably help you plan some happy times you can all enjoy. It doesn't have to be extravagant. Just a simple meal and some laughter does everyone's heart good. Enjoy your family, enjoy your friends, enjoy your food, and enjoy your work and your ministry. This is "from the hand of God" according to Solomon.

Solomon also instructs us to find enjoyment in our toil. Our work isn't a curse; it is a blessing from God. Whether you work for money at a full-time paid position or your "work" is like mine on a full-time volunteer basis, take enjoyment from your work. Find the joy in each task. Ask God to bless the relationships at work and in your ministry with those who labor alongside you. Don't let your work steal your joy. If you are working consistently 60-70 hours a week, you might need to stop and take a long look at how you are spending your life. While we are to enjoy our work, we can't let it take over our lives. Find the balance in your work and if you can't do that in your current line of employment, it might be time to find another job or find a way to cut back on your hours at work. Sit down with your family and discuss how to make a change in the way things are done. Life is just too short to live for your work.

Another way to get the most joy out of life is to share God's gifts with those around you. The best investment you'll ever make is to generously sow your resources into God's kingdom by helping others, and it will bring you more joy than you could imagine. Two couples who are our good friends have sold their houses in the city and moved out into the Texas countryside. We visited one of the couples for a few days to work on writing these books in a peaceful, restful place. It was better than we thought it would be. This family epitomizes what it means to enjoy life in a God-honoring way and to share God's blessings. They made it so easy for us to balance working hard on the books and taking breaks to breathe fresh country air. They have used their resources to create a haven of rest and as a place to allow others to experience God's creation. The cottage where we stayed was filled with God's presence and had every convenience we needed. Sitting by the firepit one night making s'mores, gazing up at the stars and hearing the bullfrogs' symphony, we were filled with amazement at how this couple is the perfect example for us of how to enjoy life and help others enjoy it, too. We're both a little too serious, and whether they knew it or not, they mentored us during those days on their farm in the fine art of having fun.

In your Winter Season, whether it is temporary or a permanent condition, joy is one of the critical ways to get through it in victory. This doesn't mean you have to be happy about difficult events swirling around you or about the grief you are processing, but there can be moments of joy even while you're going through it. For a few minutes each day, look for joy and you'll find it in the simplest things of life. "The joy of the Lord is our strength" is an oft-quoted Scripture. We find it printed on coffee mugs and tea towels, but the context for the verse might surprise you.

Read the back story behind it in Nehemiah 8:5-12.

⁵Ezra opened the book. All the people could see him because he was standing above them; and as he opened it, the people all stood up. ⁶Ezra praised the Lord, the great God; and all the people lifted their hands and responded, "Amen! Amen!" Then they bowed down and worshiped the Lord with their faces to the ground. ⁷The Levites—Jeshua, Bani, Sherebiah, Jamin, Akkub, Shabbethai, Hodiah, Maaseiah, Kelita, Azariah, Jozabad, Hanan and Pelaiah—instructed the people in the Law while the people were standing there. ⁸They read from the Book of the Law of God, making it clear and giving the meaning so that the people understood what was being read.

⁹Then Nehemiah the governor, Ezra the priest and teacher of the Law, and the Levites who were instructing the people said to them all, "This day is holy to the Lord your God. Do not mourn or weep." For all the people had been weeping as they listened to the words of the Law. ¹⁰Nehemiah said, "Go and enjoy choice food and sweet drinks, and send some to those who have nothing prepared. This day is holy to our Lord. Do not grieve, for the joy of the Lord is your strength."

¹¹The Levites calmed all the people, saying, "Be still, for this is a holy day. Do not grieve." ¹²Then all the people went away to eat and drink, to send portions of food and to celebrate with great joy, because they now understood the words that had been made known to them.

What three things were the Israelites to do instead of grieve?

Finish the last sentence of this verse, "for the joy _____

_____ ."

The wall around Jerusalem had been rebuilt under the leadership of Nehemiah, the governor, and Ezra, the scribe. They built a platform so these men could read Scripture all day in the hearing of the people. When the people heard the Word of God, they were cut to the heart and convicted of sin. They began to weep and mourn, but their leaders stopped them. "It's time to celebrate, not mourn!" Joy that comes from God is pure and holy and gives you spiritual, mental and physical strength.

The Bible is full of instruction in finding joy.
Read Psalm 5:11.
But let all who take refuge in you rejoice; let them ever sing for joy, and spread your protection over them, that those who love your name may exult in you.

Read Psalm 16:11.
You make known to me the path of life; in your presence there is fullness of joy; at your right hand are pleasures forevermore.

Read Psalm 19:8.
The precepts of the Lord are right, giving joy to the heart. The commands of the Lord are radiant, giving light to the eyes.

Read Psalm 32:11.
Be glad in the LORD, and rejoice, O righteous, and shout for joy, all you upright in heart!

Read Psalm 35:27, 28.
²⁷Let those who delight in my righteousness shout for joy and be glad and say evermore, "Great is the LORD, who delights in the welfare of his servant!" ²⁸ Then my tongue shall tell of your righteousness and of your praise all the day long.

Read Psalm 95:1.
Come, let us sing for joy to the Lord; let us shout aloud to the Rock of our salvation.

How many times do you see the words "joy," "rejoice," "glad," "delight" or "pleasure" in each passage above?

In these verses, what is the reason for joy?

According to these verses, how can we express our joy in the Lord?

The Psalmist tells us the reason for joy is the Lord Himself. We rejoice because of His goodness. According to these verses, our joy does not depend on our circumstances. When our joy is in the Lord, then no matter what is happening around us, we can find our delight in Him. While your circumstances may be challenging or plunging you into grief, you can draw out of the well of joy that comes from being in a loving relationship with the Lord. Solomon knew from his early years what it was like to experience joy in the Lord.

Read I Chronicles 29:22.
They ate and drank with great joy in the presence of the LORD that day. Then they acknowledged Solomon son of David as king a second time, anointing him before the LORD to be ruler and Zadok to be priest.

Read II Chronicles 7:10.
On the twenty-third day of the seventh month he sent the people to their homes, joyful and glad in heart for the good things the Lord had done for David and Solomon and for his people Israel.

Years ago, I was told by more than one Sunday School teacher that JOY means "Jesus," then "Others," then "You." While we now know that we must love and take care of ourselves as well, the old Sunday School adage is still true. You will have "joy, joy, joy, joy down in your heart to stay when you have the love of Jesus in your heart" and then give it away.

A Bit of Wisdom

If you're an in-town grandparent, joy can be found in making a big deal of the grandchildren's performances. Buy tickets on the front row, bring them flowers and celebrate their achievements. Don't miss their ballgames. If you have a zoo or museum in your city, see if it's possible to buy a year-long pass and take your younger grandchildren often! If you're an out-of-town grandparent, work at face-to-face communication with your phone. Mail them Valentines, birthday and Christmas cards. Plan to visit as often as you can and make it easy on their parents.

If you don't have grandchildren and are not in that stage of life, look around and find someone who needs to be adopted! Are there neighbor children who need your love? Do you have an elderly neighbor who needs a friend? What about your teenager's best friend or the kid who is always asking for a ride home? Start praying and asking the Lord to open your eyes to see those around you who need your care. Bringing people into your life who need your love can be an untapped source of joy!

Gifts of Wisdom, Knowledge and Joy

Day 5

Father God, I bow my heart and mind before Your throne. You are great and greatly to be praised. There is no one like You in heaven or on earth. Your sovereignty covers the earth, and I submit to Your will. Lord, thank You for loving me. I want to tell You how much I love You. Today as I study Your Word, drive it deep into my heart. Convict me of sin, encourage my faith, and spur me on to good works. I pray all this in the powerful name that is above every name, the name of Jesus. Amen.

ABIGAIL loved the Lord, and she loved her mom. She and her mother used to get up early in the morning before the sun came up and with coffee cups in hand, they shared their latest revelation from the Lord. It was one of the sweetest memories Abigail had of her mother. Her mom taught her to pray Scriptural prayers based on God's Word. Abby and her mother prayed over each family member, and she could feel the electricity in the air as they prayed. Her parents had little in the way of material goods, but they were the richest people on earth in the important things.

Mom had the gift of wisdom, and all of her five daughters used to call her regularly to drink from that fountain. She seemed to have unusual perception about the knottiest problems they faced. She was a life-long learner. She read voraciously from many authors and kept up with current events all over the world to increase her knowledge. She was an amazing woman, and they all looked up to her. But most amazing of all about their mother was her internal well-spring of joy. Joy bubbled up from her easy laughter and lit the wrinkles around her eyes.

Strangely, things just came to Mom, even from people who were opposed to her beliefs. Mom and Dad's next-door neighbors were devoted atheists and regularly let their views be known. Mom never preached to them but was a loving and friendly neighbor. The couple were avid gardeners and tilled their large backyard lot into a productive vegetable garden. It never failed that when their crop was ripe for the picking of one vegetable or another, they had to leave town and asked Mom and Dad to harvest what was ready and keep it for themselves. Mom and Dad ate the finest organic produce around. Things like that happened to them all the time.

Read Ecclesiastes 2:26.
For to the one who pleases him, God has given wisdom and knowledge and joy, but to the sinner he has given the business of gathering and collecting, only to give to one who pleases God. This also is vanity and a striving after wind.

❋ What does it mean to "please God?"

What three gifts has God given to those who please Him?

To the sinner, God has given the task of _____ and _____ to supply those who please Him.

This verse was Solomon's personal experience. He had learned early in his life that by asking for wisdom, it pleased God. And God bestowed on him more wisdom, knowledge and the accompanying joy than he could have ever imagined.

Re-read II Chronicles 1:10-12.
¹⁰Give me now wisdom and knowledge to go out and come in before this people, for who can govern this people of yours, which is so great?" ¹¹God answered Solomon, "Because this was in your heart, and you have not asked for possessions, wealth, honor, or the life of those who hate you, and have not even asked for long life, but have asked for wisdom and knowledge for yourself that you may govern my people over whom I have made you king, ¹²wisdom and knowledge are granted to you. I will also give you riches, possessions, and honor, such as none of the kings had who were before you, and none after you shall have the like."

Solomon knew that these gifts come from a life that's walking in harmony with God. So, he knew what it felt like to be given these gifts of wisdom, knowledge, and joy. The key phrase of Ecclesiastes 2:26 is "For to the one who pleases him…" So how do we please God so that we can receive the gifts of wisdom, knowledge, and joy? Paul teaches us in his letter to the Romans.

Read Romans 12:1, 2.
¹Therefore, I urge you, brothers and sisters, in view of God's mercy, to offer your bodies as a living sacrifice, holy and pleasing to God—this is your true and proper worship. ²Do not conform to the pattern of this world, but be transformed by the renewing of your mind. Then you will be able to test and approve what God's will is—his good, pleasing and perfect will.

Paul instructs us to offer our body to God in three ways:

1.

2.

3.

How does Paul use the words "conform" and "transform?"

✹ How does pleasing God affect knowing His will?

You don't need to behave perfectly to please God. You don't need to do penance to get into God's good graces. God loves you unconditionally and completely, and your behavior doesn't alter that fact. He is looking at your heart. God is looking for people who will offer themselves to Him, sacrificing their own agenda and worshiping Him with pure hearts. He calls us to be transformed by minds that are renewed in His Word. The reason it pleases Him when we don't conform to the world is because that path destroys us. He is pleased when we seek His will and do it because it brings us life! God wants to give you the gifts of wisdom, knowledge and joy and you will discover those gifts when you walk in a way pleasing to Him.

For more instruction about how to please God, read I Timothy 5:3-5.
³Give proper recognition to those widows who are really in need. ⁴But if a widow has children or grandchildren, these should learn first of all to put their religion into practice by caring for their own family and so repaying their parents and grandparents, for this is pleasing to God. ⁵The widow who is really in need and left all alone puts her hope in God and continues night and day to pray and to ask God for help.

What does this passage tell us about pleasing God?

How can you put this passage into practice?

Now let's move on to the next part of Ecclesiastes 2:26. Solomon saw that God bestows three gifts on those who please Him. He gives wisdom to realize that tangible pleasures of this life are to be enjoyed and shared, not hoarded nor obsessed over; He gives knowledge to realize that life is fleeting, and we should use our blessings to do good now in our own generation; and He gives deep, abiding joy as we live life fully with open arms and open hearts.

In contrast, according to Solomon in Ecclesiastes 2:26, to those who walk in darkness God has given the job of "gathering and collecting" that which will be turned over to His own. We see several examples of this phenomenon in biblical history. In ancient Egypt, Pharaoh's learned men trained Moses, educating him in the highest degree of Egyptian knowledge while he was living in the palace. He then took that knowledge to organize and lead all of Pharaoh's Hebrew slaves away to build a new nation.

Read Exodus 12:35, 36.
35 The Israelites did as Moses instructed and asked the Egyptians for articles of silver and gold and for clothing. 36 The Lord had made the Egyptians favorably disposed toward the people, and they gave them what they asked for; so they plundered the Egyptians.

How did the Egyptians give up their possessions to God's chosen people?

As they left Egypt, the Lord caused the Egyptians to turn over their possessions to His people, supplying all of their needs. They even gave up their gold and silver, which was later used to build the ark and the elements for the tabernacle. At another time in Israel's history, God caused an idolatrous people group to provide for His children.

Read Deuteronomy 11: 23-25.
23 Then the Lord will drive out all these nations before you, and you will dispossess nations greater and mightier than you. 24 Every place on which the sole of your foot treads shall be yours. Your territory shall be from the wilderness to the Lebanon and from the River, the river Euphrates, to the western sea. 25 No one shall be able to stand against you. The Lord your God will lay the fear of you and the dread of you on all the land that you shall tread, as he promised you.

How did God cleanse the land and provide for His people with one move?

The Canaanites tilled the soil and planted the crops and vineyards, preparing everything that would eventually be turned over to the Israelites when they were ready to take possession of the promised land under Joshua. God provides for His own and causes "all things to work together for their good."

God's gifts to those who please Him are wisdom, knowledge and JOY! Take some time today to listen to Rend Collective's "The Joy of the Lord" on YouTube. You might also like to listen to the classic "Joyful, joyful we adore Thee" as you read the words below.

1. Joyful, joyful, we adore Thee, God of glory, Lord of love; Hearts unfold like flow'rs before Thee, Op'ning to the sun above. Melt the clouds of sin and sadness; Drive the dark of doubt away; Giver of immortal gladness, Fill us with the light of day!

2. All Thy works with joy surround Thee, Earth and heav'n reflect Thy rays, Stars and angels sing around Thee, Center of unbroken praise. Field and forest, vale and mountain, Flow'ry meadow, flashing sea, Singing bird and flowing fountain. Call us to rejoice in Thee.

3. Thou art giving and forgiving, Ever blessing, ever blest, Wellspring of the joy of living, Ocean depth of happy rest! Thou our Father, Christ our Brother, All who live in love are Thine; Teach us how to love each other, Lift us to the joy divine.

4. Mortals, join the happy chorus, Which the morning stars began; Father love is reigning o'er us, Brother love binds man to man. Ever singing, march we onward, Victors in the midst of strife, Joyful music leads us Sunward In the triumph song of life.

A Bit of Wisdom

Joy can be found in helping others. Roll up your sleeves and help someone with house cleaning, laundry, ironing (does anyone do that anymore?), cooking or driving them to a doctor's appointment. My dad always said the best way to get out of the doldrums is to help someone else. Somehow, your heart begins to lighten when you serve.

WEEK 3
WHAT TIME IS IT?
PART 1

A Personal Message to You from Solomon

What time is it? There is a season for everything, as you will learn this week. I have learned that seasons can guide you into the rhythm of life as God intended. If you try to telescope a season or go around it, you'll only find frustration. But if you will flow with the seasons of your life, just as spring follows winter and autumn follows summer, you'll discover the joy and variation of the colorful life God has planned for you to live. He will guide you through each season where you will learn what you could not learn any other way.

New Life — Day 1

Oh Lord, our Lord, how excellent is Your name. You are King of all kings and Lord of all lords. I bow my heart, my life and my soul to You. Lord Jesus, guide me through the current season of my life. Give me the wisdom I need for these days. Thank You for never leaving nor forsaking me. I love You and thank You for your constant presence. I pray all of this in Jesus' name. Amen.

The long-awaited news came on the most ordinary day. A new life was being added to the family. Abigail sat down and held her face in her hands and wept. She couldn't remember how long she'd been praying for this baby. It felt like the newest generation of her family would never arrive. But the call from her son and daughter-in-law confirmed that she'd be a grandmother at last. Joy bubbled up from deep inside. What would it be like to hold the baby of her baby? How would she feel? Would she feel older or younger? What would this new relationship entail? How does one go about being a really wonderful grandmother?

When she shared the news with her husband, John, he didn't seem as thrilled as she'd hoped. He was okay with learning he'd been moved up a generation, but he didn't want it to curtail their travel plans or take too much time. An avid golfer, he had just retired from 43 years in the industry and felt he'd earned a well-deserved golf club membership where he planned to spend most of his time.

Abigail spent time praying out both her joy and her apprehension at the coming of the new baby. She asked God to use her in the new grandchild's life and to strengthen her marriage. Strange that after 45 years together, they were on another learning curve, navigating some new territory once again to learn how to be one in spirit and soul as they welcomed the new generation.

Read Ecclesiastes 3:1-8.

¹For everything there is a season, and a time for every matter under heaven: ²a time to be born, and a time to die; a time to plant, and a time to pluck up what is planted; ³a time to kill, and a time to heal; a time to break down, and a time to build up; ⁴a time to weep, and a time to laugh; a time to mourn, and a time to dance; ⁵a time to cast away stones, and a time to gather stones together; a time to embrace, and a time to refrain from embracing; ⁶a time to seek, and a time to lose; a time to keep, and a time to cast away; ⁷a time to tear, and a time to sew; a time to keep silence, and a time to speak; ⁸a time to love, and a time to hate; a time for war, and a time for peace.

From Ecclesiastes 3:1, 2a fill in the blanks.

¹For everything there is a_____, and a time for every matter under heaven: ²a time to be_____, and a time to_____;

The word "season" is from the Hebrew word *zeman* which means "appointed season or appointed time."[1] God not only ordained the seasons in nature, but He designed our human lives to follow certain seasons as well. Solomon, the wisest king in the world, tells us in Ecclesiastes that every part of life—from birth to death—has its own time. We can't telescope the seasons, we can't stop them, slow them, hurry them, or eliminate them. The seasons keep coming like clock-work. We can cooperate with the passages of time, the coming of new seasons, or fight it bitterly. The choice is ours. Either we will embrace the changes and, as my sister Judy says, "decide to get happy," or resist change to our own hurt.

The brilliant thing about Solomon's list of seasons is that he doesn't interpret them for us but just simply states that they are. By not telling us exactly how to interpret them, it leaves room for God to speak to us in a way we can hear His voice for our current situation. If we will read these "seasons" with a listening ear to what the Spirit wants to say to us, He will lead us into truth for today.

Life is like a library, and each season in life is like a separate book. You take down each "book" or each "season" and learn what you need from it, and when that season has passed, you put the "book" back on the shelf until you need it again. Throughout your life, you'll be checking out one "book," then another. Some of the seasons are comedies; others are tragedies. But all of them can teach us. Sometimes you'll check out more than one "book" at a time, experiencing multiple seasons at the same time, and that's when life is complicated. For example, you might be welcoming the birth of a grandchild at the same time your parents are dying. But we can learn from each season how to walk with wisdom, knowledge, grace, and eventually JOY. Solomon begins with the bookends of life: birth and death.

There is a time to be born. The addition of a new baby or new grandchild or new great-niece or nephew usually brings great joy to a family. If the young couple are in a committed, loving marriage, it makes it all the more a time of rejoicing. If they aren't married or are in a troubled relationship, a new baby can bring apprehension. Whatever the circumstances of the new baby's origin, you can be the one to embrace and welcome this new life into the world.

Read Psalm 139:13, 14.
13For you formed my inward parts; you knitted me together in my mother's womb. 14I praise you, for I am fearfully and wonderfully made. Wonderful are your works; my soul knows it very well.

✺ At what point in the birth process is a human being a person, made in God's image?

How do these verses affirm your worth?

Each child is a gift from God, made in His image. Each one is handcrafted by God in the womb to be unique, special, and gifted in various ways. Life begins at conception and is very precious. Every child deserves to know he is loved. This forms the foundation for the rest of his life. It molds and shapes how he views himself and others, and especially how he views God. It is the privilege of parents and the extended family to express God's love to each child who comes into the world. If you are a mother, aunt, grandmother or great-aunt, begin asking God now for practical ways in which to wrap each child in your family in unconditional love.

Read I Corinthians 13:1-8.
¹If I speak in the tongues of men and of angels, but have not love, I am a noisy gong or a clanging cymbal. ²And if I have prophetic powers, and understand all mysteries and all knowledge, and if I have all faith, so as to remove mountains, but have not love, I am nothing. ³If I give away all I have, and if I deliver up my body to be burned, but have not love, I gain nothing. ⁴Love is patient and kind; love does not envy or boast; it is not arrogant ⁵or rude. It does not insist on its own way; it is not irritable or resentful; ⁶it does not rejoice at wrongdoing, but rejoices with the truth. ⁷Love bears all things, believes all things, hopes all things, endures all things. ⁸Love never ends.

List the ways to express love given in this passage.

_____

_____

What are three practical ways you can start expressing love that way to a child in your family?

1.

2.

3.

Week 3: Day 1

Parenting begins a new season for a married couple. When you go from two to three, it changes the dynamic of family life. Parenting requires sacrificial love to care for a little one who cannot do anything for himself or herself. Both mother and father are needed to supply everything the baby needs to grow physically, spiritually and emotionally. You'll lose sleep, your privacy, and you'll learn to eat standing up rocking a baby. You'll take showers quickly, probably not often enough, and sleep lightly, keeping an ear open for any sound. But for couples who have the privilege to become parents, parenting is one of the most rewarding and enjoyable blessings a couple can experience. You'll discover a whole new love you never thought possible. You'll understand God's love for you in a new way.

Read Psalm 127:3-5.
³Behold, children are a heritage from the LORD, the fruit of the womb a reward. ⁴Like arrows in the hand of a warrior are the children of one's youth. ⁵Blessed is the man who fills his quiver with them!

Children are a _____.

Why are children like arrows in the hand of a warrior?

If your children have children, you'll enter a whole, new, wonderful season. Grandparenting is a new time of life with a new role. As grandparents, we have a special place in the family that is under the authority and rules of the child's parents, but is unique as someone who loves the grandkids more than life and can be more objective than the parents. The fun part of grandparenting is that you can have special things only Grandma/Auntie can do. Two of our grandchildren eat Sunday breakfast with us each week while their parents set up the church for the worship service. These kids want the same breakfast each week that they don't eat at home. That's what makes coming to Grandma's house special!

We have an entire closet in a guest bedroom dedicated to costumes for dress up. The grandchildren have created endless "shows" using them. We decorate for every holiday and have big, loud, crazy family dinners and laugh until we cry. I love my people, and I want them at my house as often as we can gather them. This is a season in life I am enjoying with all my heart. Since our first two grandchildren are already out of the nest, I can see this season coming to a close over the next few years, and I don't want to miss a minute of it!

For seven years, I did miss a lot of it. We lived in Indonesia and Australia when our grandchildren were very young, and many of them were born while we lived overseas. It was a big effort to stay connected, to visit as much as possible, and to call often. But it was so worth it. One day, when we came home to live in Houston between our international assignments, our eldest granddaughter and I were coloring together when suddenly she asked me, "How do I ask Jesus into my heart?" I had the privilege to explain the gospel to her and a few days later she accepted Christ as her Lord and Savior. God doesn't have grandchildren, only children, and it was such joy to see her become a child of God. All ten of our grandchildren have made this decision to follow Christ, and nothing could make me happier.

Parenting and grandparenting is not about babysitting but is an investment in the future of your family. As grandparents, we keep the grandkids to encourage young marriages and to help harried parents. We don't enable our children to be irresponsible, but we help ease their burdens when we can. Our goal is to produce godly offspring in the generations that follow us.

Read Deuteronomy 6:1-3.

¹Now this is the commandment—the statutes and the rules—that the LORD your God commanded me to teach you, that you may do them in the land to which you are going over, to possess it, ²that you may fear the LORD your God, you and your son and your son's son, by keeping all his statutes and his commandments, which I command you, all the days of your life, and that your days may be long. ³Hear therefore, O Israel, and be careful to do them, that it may go well with you, and that you may multiply greatly, as the LORD, the God of your fathers, has promised you, in a land flowing with milk and honey.

What is the phrase in verse 2 that refers to three generations?

What is the commandment to grandparents and parents?

Moses was thinking generationally in this passage. Look at verse 2. He was teaching us God's perspective in parenting and grandparenting. If each of us produces godly offspring, then if our children produce godly offspring with their children, we are furthering God's kingdom and His righteousness in this world. So as godly parents, we are called to create a legacy of faith through our children. That's the big picture of what family is all about.

One of the greatest gifts you can give your children and grandchildren is the gift of regular prayer. Since the goal of parenting and grandparenting is to produce godly offspring, prayer is a necessity. In the *Wisdom for Fathers and Wisdom for Mothers* books, we give 12 Scriptural prayers to pray for your children, and we know by experience how God has used those prayers in the life of our family. Now we are praying these important prayers over our grandchildren.

Your grandchildren or nieces and nephews might be in a family where they are not taken to church. Perhaps one or both of their parents aren't Christians.

Your prayers for them will have a powerful effect on their lives, and you might be the one to share the gospel with them. Perhaps, with the permission of the parents, you can involve them in a local body of Christ. If the children in your family are being raised in a Christian home, talk with them about their faith and encourage them to go on mission trips and to serve the body of Christ. Pray for them and for their future mates. Every prayer is an investment in your future.

[1] *Strong's Exhaustive Concordance of the Bible,* Hebrew Number 2165, biblehub.com.

A Bit of Wisdom

Most moms, grandmothers, and aunties love giving gifts to the children of the family. Why not think about giving experiences instead of material things? Start thinking outside the box with something like a ticket to the zoo or museum, a session of horseback riding, a trip to the nail salon or a fishing trip. You might even be able to get tickets for yourself and your kids or grandkids to your city's ballet or theater or on a special occasion, a professional game. Maybe you can even travel with your grandchildren and possibly go on a mission trip with them.

If you can afford it, you might be able to contribute to a child's, grandchild's, nephew's or niece's college fund on each birthday. In the US, there is a special investment fund that is tax deductible for a child's education, the 529 fund.

If you have significant financial resources to pass on, pray and think carefully about what you will leave your children and grandchildren in the future. The book *Splitting Heirs* by Ron Blue is a great resource to help you make wise decisions concerning inheritance and how to give now while you're still alive to enjoy it. You don't want to take away your children's motivation to work and provide for themselves, so be careful not to give too much but give enough to encourage their education and preparation for God's calling on their lives. You'll want to be generous but give with wisdom and discretion. We don't give to change their lifestyle but to help them accomplish their mission.

If you cannot help your heirs financially, you still have a lot to give the next generation. Your wisdom and knowledge, your sense of joy, your love and concern, and mostly your prayers will leave them the greatest legacy of all.

Leaving for Home — Day 2

Lord Jesus, I long for Your presence today. I sit before You quietly receiving Your love and grace. Some seasons are difficult. Thank You for always being there, whether I am having a good day or a hard one. I trust You to carry the things that are too difficult for me. Speak to me today from Your Word. Plant Your truth deep within my heart. I love You. In Jesus' name I pray. Amen.

As much as the five daughters loved each other, they loved their parents even more. Their strong father and their fun-loving mother had created a nest for the girls where they grew up in safety and unconditional love. Each daughter was celebrated for her unique gifts and abilities. This family laughed together, prayed together, cried together and worked together for God's kingdom and for future generations.

But things were changing with Mom and Dad. Their forgetfulness was becoming pronounced and troublesome. Medications weren't taken on time, doctors' appointments were missed, bills were left unpaid for the first time in their lives, and what about their driving? All of the daughters worried and fussed over their elderly parents. It was time for a family meeting. As the girls talked about who would and could do which part of elder care, it became obvious how they would split the duties. Some of them had more time or natural ability to complete tasks that were more hands-on, like medical appointments and financial bookkeeping. Some were committed to daily visits and phone calls. Each had her part.

For several months, their system was working. Mom and Dad were receiving the right amount of care and seemed to be functioning so much better. Then the day of the dreaded emergency call came. Dad had fallen and broken a hip, and all the plans had to be scrapped and rearranged to provide hospitalization and rehabilitation for Dad, all the while caring for Mom, who was suffering more and more from dementia.

Mom's care became as much of a concern as Dad's, but they were on such different care levels now. More phone meetings and text messages between the sisters established a new routine of care. Dad began to slowly recover, and Mom seemed to be accepting his absence from home and enjoying her long visits with him in the hospital.

For a whole year, things fell into a new rhythm. While it was more stressful for the daughters, and their phone meetings and chats via texts were happening now almost daily, sometimes hourly, they were making it through the challenges of working with medical staff, moving Mom and Dad into a care facility where Dad could receive the rehabilitation he needed and Mom had the memory care she needed. The in-town daughters shouldered the daily visits and laundry duties, while the out-of-town sisters did the finances and communication with medical staff. It felt to the girls as if they were walking on eggshells with their parent's care, as it was hard to know what to do to love and honor them and take the best care of them. All five of them slept with their phones under their pillows for an entire year, awaiting a call at any minute that would send them rushing back for more care.

Then suddenly when all seemed to be going well, Dad's health made a downward spiral. An infection settled in the hip, followed by pneumonia, and he was losing ground fast. The daughters all came rushing home to be with their beloved father and to care for Mom who was bewildered, sad, and confused. It became obvious that Dad would not recover. After two weeks of slow and steady decline, the end was near. The girls gathered around his bed and for 36 hours sang hymns, cried, prayed, told their Dad how much they loved him, told funny stories of his wonderful life, and rehearsed for him again how much he meant to them. And the moment finally came when there was no more breath, no more heart sounds, and the room became incredibly quiet.

Read Ecclesiastes 3:1, 2.
¹For everything there is a season, and a time for every matter under heaven: ²a time to be born, and a time to die.

Fill in the blank: "a time to be born and a time to _____."

Winter Season can also bring death. It's a subject most of us avoid until it's unavoidable. Either you or your loved one may be facing death or the dying process even now. Perhaps in the early days, there was the feeling something wasn't "right." The symptoms couldn't be ignored any more. The tests were made, the diagnosis given, the treatment options explained. But your heart cries out, "No!"

Read Psalm 89:47, 48.
⁴⁷Remember how short my time is! For what vanity you have created all the children of man! ⁴⁸What man can live and never see death? Who can deliver his soul from the power of Sheol?

What inevitability does the Psalmist face?

Solomon acknowledged that life is short and that death comes to everyone. He asked who can deliver us from "sheol." The Hebrew word "sheol" means the grave—the place to which people go at death. The King James Version of the Bible translates this word "the hand of the grave" in Ps. 89:48. In other words, it is just a way to say, "death," and not specifically heaven or hell.

Read Psalm 103:14-18.
¹⁴For he knows our frame; he remembers that we are dust. ¹⁵As for man, his days are like grass; he flourishes like a flower of the field; ¹⁶for the wind passes over it, and it is gone, and its place knows it no more. ¹⁷But the steadfast love of the LORD is from everlasting to everlasting on those who fear him, and his righteousness to children's children, ¹⁸to those who keep his covenant and remember to do his commandments.

What season of life is David describing?

✺ What stays the same even while our bodies decline and aging is taking place?

✺ After we are gone, who is comforted by God's love and righteousness?

Death is a reality for us all. The only time we are guaranteed is right now, this day. While our bodies will break down, get sick, turn gray, and eventually die, God's love is constant. His love is from everlasting in the ages past to everlasting in the future. There is nothing else like God's love. It is who He is. And that force of love is what sustains us from cradle to grave. Our response to that love is to enter into and remain in covenant relationship with Him until our last breath. It is to keep the straightforward, simple commandments He gave us: boundaries to protect us, to bless us, and for us to bless others.

Just a few weeks before my mother went to heaven, I was visiting her and started crying, so sad that I knew she would soon be leaving me. I thought my heart would break. She looked deeply at me with her blue eyes flashing and said, "When I leave this earth, only my body will leave. My love will never leave you because LOVE NEVER FAILS!!! God is LOVE, and love is everlasting. My love will always be with you." God's love and the love of our loved ones doesn't end at death. While we miss them, their love does not leave us.

Psalm 116:1-9, 15.
¹I love the LORD, because he has heard my voice and my pleas for mercy. ²Because he inclined his ear to me, therefore I will call on him as long as I live. ³The snares of death encompassed me; the pangs of Sheol laid hold on me; I suffered distress and anguish. ⁴Then I called on the name of the LORD: "O LORD, I pray, deliver my soul!" ⁵Gracious is the LORD, and righteous; our God is merciful. ⁶The LORD preserves the simple; when I was brought low, he saved me. ⁷Return, O my soul, to your rest; for the LORD has dealt bountifully with you. ⁸For you have delivered my soul from death, my eyes from tears, my feet from stumbling; ⁹I will walk before the LORD in the land of the living.

¹⁵Precious in the sight of the LORD is the death of his saints.

Which verses in this Psalm assure you that God hears your cries?

What is the first thing David does when he sees his impending death?

✺ David does some "self-talk" in verse 7. What does he tell himself when he is distressed and afraid of dying?

Fill in the blanks of Psalm 116:15.

Precious in the _____ is the

_____ of his saints.

David reminds us to cry out to the Lord when we are afraid of death. The Bible doesn't shy away from the fact that impending death brings distress and anguish.

WEEK 3: DAY 2

Death is unnatural. God designed us for eternal life, and something within us knows that death is wrong. The fall of man brought death into God's Eden. But King David begins to say to himself, "Self (or "Soul"), calm down and return to that state of rest in God. He has always dealt bountifully with you, and He's not going to stop now." David knows that God will deliver his soul from death. Note that he doesn't say God will deliver his body from death. Bodies are earth suits that are disposable. They don't last. They decline and eventually disintegrate. They are made of dust and return to dust. But our souls and spirits live forever. And because David has a personal relationship with God his Father, he knows his soul is safe even if his body is not.

When facing the decline of your parents, spouse, child or siblings or perhaps even your own death, decisions have to be made and soul-searching begins if the process is slow and over time. Dying may still seem far away, and perhaps there is hope of survival. Then the day comes when the heart must accept that the body is loosening its hold on life. It may happen over many years or a few months. This is the time to celebrate a life well-lived, to finish tasks and bring completion to life. There will be more soul-searching on the part of the dying as well as the caregiver. There will be a greater appreciation of life. Authors Gerald Dieter Griffin and Pam Umann have written a resource for those who are dying and their caregivers in *The Last Day of Winter*. Using the seasons in nature to describe the dying process, they articulate how we can best help our loved ones who are dying and how to process our own deaths, not living in denial, but facing and embracing this season of life that comes to all.

For those loved ones who do not have a personal relationship with Jesus, this is an important opportunity to share your faith with them—not to be pushy or judgmental but to share the good news of Jesus with them and the joy and purpose of knowing Him personally. Ask the Lord to give you just the right words to bring the Truth to your loved one.

If the dying season is extended, it a time of celebrating life and the insights gained from lifelong experiences and the wisdom collected along the way. It's best to enjoy that reflection while the dying one is still here to participate. Don't wait until the funeral or memorial service to talk about the wonderful adventures and insightful words of the one who is moving from this world to the next.

There are emotional symptoms of dying. Depression is a natural and sometimes pivotal time in the dying process for the one dying as well as for the caregiver but of course, it is the most difficult. As the person and his caregivers accept the reality of life nearing its end, it is sad and hard, and no one can really make that easier. It is not helpful to pull out Bible verses and quote pithy sayings at such a time, trying to make the depression go away. Your ministry of presence as a caregiver is the best thing you can do. Just BE THERE. You don't have to talk or say anything wise. You don't need to bustle around doing things. Just be still, be there, drink a coffee or sip tea and if the dying one wants to talk, listen attentively without judgment (Don't say, "I told you to stop smoking years ago," or "You should have been exercising more.") or any other type of criticism. Pray with them when that seems appropriate, but even your prayers need to be focused on Jesus and His love, not crying and begging for healing when it's obvious the Lord is taking your loved one home.

We say those words…taking our loved ones "home." But it doesn't feel like home. It feels like loss, pain, abandonment, grief. Sometimes you grieve your loved one while they are still with you. It's okay, and in fact, it's best to let the grief happen. Let it come in. Don't push it away. You need to go through this, not around it. Allow yourself the tears or no tears. Allow yourself to feel the pain of impending separation and, at times, allow yourself to feel nothing but numbness. I'm not advocating that you wallow in grief in a prolonged, unhealthy way; but we must give ourselves permission to be sad, to cry, to be angry at the loss, to wail, and to hurt.

Others may experience the sudden, shocking, untimely death of a loved one. It is so different from the expected death of someone close to you. One of my friends experienced both kinds of loss in less than two years. Her mother's death was very much like the loss of my parents and happened when her mother was elderly and ready to go to heaven. She had time to hold her hand, minister and love on her, reminisce, adjust to the inevitable loss, and tell her goodbye.

But the death of her husband was traumatic. She was standing in the kitchen, talking to him at lunch; and 30 minutes later she was holding him in her arms, trying to give him CPR, denying the fact that he was already dead. It was a tremendous shock and took a long time to absorb.

How can we prepare for that? The most important way is to maintain a loving, forgiving, accepting relationship with those we love. We need to tell them often that we love them unconditionally. My friend tells me she can truly say that she and her children had no regrets in their relationship with their husband and father. How she wished she could have held his hand and told him once more how much she loved him, how proud she was to be his wife, and how she looked forward to being reunited with him in heaven. She didn't get to say goodbye, but she has the peace of knowing it is never goodbye; it is "see you later."

After experiences such as these, you'll sometimes need what I call a "Pajama Day" where you "cocoon" by climbing in bed or curling up on the couch, wrapping in a warm blanket, putting on instrumental praise music, and taking a nap. You might light candles, have your favorite coffee or tea, and watch a good movie. Give yourself space and time to heal. Don't do anything. Give yourself a complete break. It's okay not to be okay.

We have sanitized death and isolated it from life. Our great-grandparents died at home in bed with all the family gathered around. Death used to be part of the normal rhythm of life, where children were present at the death of their grandparents and learned to accept the dying process.

They learned to cry and mourn the loss of a loved one and then to let go and begin to live again. It's time to bring death back into the experience of our children and grandchildren. To help them learn that we are not our bodies. We are spirit beings who temporarily live in earth suits that are disposable. And when the time comes to dispose of our bodies, we can celebrate the great time we had in them and then kiss them goodbye.

Read Psalm 23:4.
*⁴Even though I walk through the valley of the shadow of **death**, I will fear no evil, for you are with me; your rod and your staff, they comfort me.*

A Bit of Wisdom

One friend, whose husband suddenly died, decided that for her family it was important to replace the traumatic memories of the day of his death with joyful and happy ones. She made the decision to sell his car that was sitting in her driveway (and causing painful memories every time she saw it) and use the money from the sale to take her children and grandchildren on a fun-filled vacation. They set the date for the trip for the first anniversary of his death to be together, celebrating his life. While the trip was a time for many tears to be shed over the loss of this amazing husband and father, it was comforting to be together to share in their grief and then to wipe away their tears and make new memories at a celebration dinner in his honor.

Planting and Plucking Up

Day 3

Heavenly Father, teach me how to let go of things I need to release and to hold on to only those things that have eternal value. Help me to understand the season I am in now and not to cling to what is in the past. Lord, I want to live freely, not weighed down by baggage that needs to be unpacked and left behind. Give me the grace and strength I need to clean out, clear out, sort out the essentials and only keep in my life what is best. I can't go through this process without Your wisdom and insight. So, Lord, flood the eyes of my heart with light. Set me free from fear. Show me the way. In Jesus' name I pray, Amen.

AFTER THEIR FATHER'S MEMORIAL SERVICE, it was clear something had to be done about Mom and Dad's house. It had 60 years of memories and memorabilia that needed sorting, distributing, and cleaning out. It was a mammoth task. Two sisters set to work, setting aside first those things that were priceless and precious to the family. Those would need to be divided equally among the five families since all of the daughters were sentimental about these things. There was only one problem. Mom and Dad had few possessions that were really worth anything to anyone outside of the family, but there was one special piece of furniture that all five girls wanted. It had come down to the family through generations from the old country. Stories abounded about how it was used and by whom. It had both sentimental and monetary value. How would they divide it? They finally decided they would share it by placing it first in one sister's house then, after a few years, it would move to the next house and so on, until everyone had a turn with the lovely piece.

The task of dividing, sorting and transporting all of the goods from their parents' home took months of hard work. Madeline and Luke took everything they could to their mission. There still seemed to be a houseful of memories, necessities, and some downright rubbish. The sisters worked for several more months, sometimes together, sometimes individually. There were tears, memories shared, bagging up, hauling out the contents of two lives very well lived and loved. Then came the business of selling, giving away, and throwing away the rest. They could finally put the house on the market. When buyers came quickly, it was another jolt to say goodbye to the house they'd loved so long and with so many happy memories.

Read Ecclesiastes 3:1-3.
¹For everything there is a season, and a time for every matter under heaven: ²a time to be born, and a time to die; a time to plant, and a time to pluck up what is planted; ³a time to kill, and a time to heal; a time to break down, and a time to build up;

List the "times" listed in these verses:

A time to _____.

A time to _____.

A time to _____.

A time to _____.

A time to _____.

A time to _____.

A time to _____.

A time to _____.

What are the contrasts in this passage?

✺ What in your life needs to be "planted" or started?

✺ How does it make you feel to think about a "time to pluck up what is planted?"

We plant gardens and trees, plant ideas, plant our feet, and plant churches. What has God called you to plant in this season? Perhaps God has put it on your heart to start a new ministry or even a new church in an area where there are no churches. Maybe you need to plant your feet in a community and take ownership of ministering to your neighbors. You might want to plant some ideas in the hearts of your children or grandchildren to give them vision for their future. Ask God what He wants you to plant in this season of your life.

Winter Season, for some, can be a time of "plucking up what was planted." This can be a time of harvesting what was planted at another time or by someone else. It is time to reap what has been sown. But there is another kind of "plucking up." It might be a time of getting rid of the old to make way for the new. Births or deaths, job change or the empty nest, a child starting a new school, retirement or illness, the marriage of your child or a move are a time to ask some important questions: What is it time to let go of in my life right now, either temporarily or permanently? What is new around the corner just waiting to happen if I clear out some space in my life?

What can you let go?

___

What do you need to clean out?

___

The most important kind of "plucking up what is planted" is getting rid of anything in your life that distracts you from walking with the Lord. If something has become an idol, it's time for it to go. We read in II Chronicles how King Hezekiah did a cleansing of God's temple to do just that.

Read II Chronicles 29:1-12, 15, 16, 18, 19.
¹Hezekiah began to reign when he was twenty-five years old, and he reigned twenty-nine years in Jerusalem. His mother's name was Abijah the daughter of Zechariah. ²And he did what was right in the eyes of the LORD, according to all that David his father had done. ³In the first year of his reign, in the first month, he opened the doors of the house of the LORD and repaired them. ⁴He brought in the priests and the Levites and assembled them in the square on the east ⁵and said to them, "Hear me, Levites! Now consecrate yourselves, and consecrate the house of the LORD, the God of your fathers, and carry out the filth from the Holy Place.

⁶For our fathers have been unfaithful and have done what was evil in the sight of the LORD our God. They have forsaken him and have turned away their faces from the habitation of the LORD and turned their backs. ⁷They also shut the doors of the vestibule and put out the lamps and have not burned incense or offered burnt offerings in the Holy Place to the God of Israel. ⁸Therefore the wrath of the LORD came on Judah and Jerusalem, and he has made them an object of horror, of astonishment, and of hissing, as you see with your own eyes. ⁹For behold, our fathers have fallen by the sword, and our sons and our daughters and our wives are in captivity for this. ¹⁰Now it is in my heart to make a covenant with the LORD, the God of Israel, in order that his fierce anger may turn away from us. ¹¹My sons, do not now be negligent, for the LORD has chosen you to stand in his presence, to minister to him and to be his ministers and make offerings to him."

¹²Then the Levites arose…¹⁵gathered their brothers and consecrated themselves and went in as the king had commanded, by the words of the LORD, to cleanse the house of the LORD. ¹⁶The priests went into the inner part of the house of the LORD to cleanse it, and they brought out all the uncleanness that they found in the temple of the LORD into the court of the house of the LORD. And the Levites took it and carried it out to the brook Kidron.

¹⁸Then they went in to Hezekiah the king and said, "We have cleansed all the house of the LORD, the altar of burnt offering and all its utensils, and the table for the showbread and all its utensils. ¹⁹All the utensils that King Ahaz discarded in his reign when he was faithless, we have made ready and consecrated, and behold, they are before the altar of the LORD."

How long into his reign did Hezekiah wait to cleanse the temple?

Why did King Hezekiah have the Levites and priests cleanse it?

What can you do to consecrate yourself and your own house or apartment as a place of worship?

When you "pluck up" and lighten the load of "stuff" in your house, it lightens the load in your mind and heart, too. You want to be able to do what God is calling you to do for as long as you live. That might be just a visit one day to a different neighborhood in your city to bring the light of Jesus or to a whole other country awaiting your testimony. Plant yourself, your life—not just your money and prayers—into sharing the gospel. What gifts do you have to invest into God's kingdom?

Jesus showed us by example that there are times to "pluck up" by doing a radical clean-out and a realignment of priorities.

Read Matthew 21:12, 13.
¹²And Jesus entered the temple and drove out all who sold and bought in the temple, and he overturned the tables of the money-changers and the seats of those who sold pigeons. ¹³He said to them, "It is written, 'My house shall be called a house of prayer,' but you make it a den of robbers."

What did Jesus clean out in this passage?

What can you learn from verse 13 about the spiritual atmosphere of your own home?

Jesus was quoting Isaiah 56:7. *"These I will bring to my holy mountain, and make them joyful in my house of prayer; their burnt offerings and their sacrifices will be accepted on my altar; for my house shall be called a house of prayer for all peoples."*

Walk through your house or apartment and ask yourself, "Could I have a prayer meeting here in any room of this home?" If there are inappropriate items that would embarrass you if the pastor came for a visit, then why not discard them now? By doing a prayer walk inside your home, dedicate each room for His honor and glory.

In any transition, like the beginning of the school year, retirement, divorce, the death of a loved one, a move or health issues, it is a good time to "pluck up" those things that are tying you down. It might be realizing you have too many material possessions. It could be just mountains of out-of-date clothing bulging in your closets or the dishes in the cupboard you no longer use or need. It might be a garage full of things that were useful 20 years ago but have long since collected dust and fallen into disrepair. This is the time of your life where some tidying up will make a huge difference. When you become a lean machine, you'll be able to go where God wants you to go and do what God wants you to do.

If you are a senior adult, you can experience the joy of "plucking up what is planted" by handing down family treasures now instead of waiting for your children to dispose and disperse all of your belongings after your death. Why not get in on the fun of surprising some of your heirs with treasures from your house now? Christmas and birthdays can become a special time of sharing precious things from the past, perhaps some items that have been passed down for generations. Giving the history of the object and a connection to the present can turn ordinary things into treasures. It's a way to pass on the oral traditions of your family heritage with something tangible for the newer generations to identify and remember. The year my parents died, I was sentimental about everything that had passed to me from their home because of my strong bond with both of them and the happy memories triggered by each small item. It took a while for me to become objective about these objects. So, give yourself time in making decisions to save or let go.

I did something the Christmas after my parents were gone that is funny now, but at the time in my sentimental state felt right. Now in hindsight, I realize my sentiments weren't always shared. I gave each child and grandchild a hymnal from my father's extensive collection, even cutting out his signature from cancelled checks and gluing them into the opening pages. My adult children appreciated these old books, but when my five-year-old grandson opened his hymnal, not understanding what it was or who had owned it, he was disappointed to say the very least. The next year, if you can believe it, he remembered the gift. Bracing himself for the worst, he pointed to a wrapped gift under my tree and asked me if I was going to give him another "Bible book," as he called it, for Christmas. I assured him there would be no more ancient books for him under my tree! So use discretion when giving old treasures!

Sometimes the reason we hold onto our things is because we haven't realized we're in a new season of life that requires a different way of living. Think outside the box if you're in a transitional Winter Season like empty nest or retirement to see where you live now and where you want to live. Assess how much you really need to function daily, what you could easily do without, and what you need surrounding you to bring enjoyment to life.

"Plucking up what is planted" can also refer to moving from one location to another. You might need a new place for your family to thrive because you have outgrown your current living situation. Or perhaps God is calling you to live in a new city, and you need to pull up stakes and make the move. For those in the active retirement phase of a Winter Season, you'll be making decisions about retirement, living prayerfully and carefully with your ultimate goal in mind: to bring God glory and honor until the end of your days. Where does God want you to live? What is best for your family? How can you make a difference by investing in others at this stage of life? How close should you or could you live to your children and grandchildren to make an impact and help them, and later, for them to help you?

Some retired couples have dreamed of living on the lake or in the mountains and after selling the family home, move to their dream location only to realize they are too far from their children, grandchildren, church and friends. After a couple of years, they often move back to their home area where long-standing relationships and deep ties mean more than the scenery. Some couples do move, taking the opportunity of the empty nest and retirement to move to a new place where they intentionally share the gospel. Others temporarily take the place of a missionary or pastor, giving them the sabbatical rest they need. A short-term move to an international location with purpose can be just the right adventure for this new stage of life.

Downsizing might be the right solution or it might not. David and I are empty-nesters, but because our children and grandchildren live nearby and we have many international friends who visit, having a house too small to accommodate large family and ministry gatherings would not work for us. We're not ready yet to move to a smaller home, but someday, I'm sure we will be. For now, we're trying to clear out and clean out excess clutter in our house and in our lives. We want to be ready for whatever God calls us to do next in this amazing season.

A Bit of Wisdom

If you don't know where to start on your house-cleaning, try watching a video on Netflix or YouTube that will give step-by-step instructions on cleaning out and letting go. It might be a painful process for you, but you'll love the way you'll feel when it's finished. And you'll be freed from things in your past that need to be left in the past.

Time to Kill — Day 4

Lord, create in me a clean heart. Wash away the blockage in my life that keeps me from intimacy with You. Please forgive me for holding onto selfish desires and behaviors that hurt myself and others. Break off those things that keep me in bondage. Lord, I want to worship You in Spirit and in truth. Lead me every step of the way. Here is my heart. I pray this now in Jesus' name. Amen.

MADELINE was getting ready for the annual mission convention. There were an inordinate number of pastors' wives and missionary women who were really beautiful. That wasn't a bad thing…until Madeline looked in the mirror. She just didn't measure up. She knew she should be spiritually mature enough not to care, but honestly, she did. She hated this about herself—constantly comparing her looks to other women. That didn't seem right for a missionary; and of course, she didn't tell anyone about her private battle, but there it was. What was she to do about this glaring issue in her heart? She so wanted to be free to focus on God's will, on the great sermons that would be preached at the meetings, and to enter into worship. But with her focus on her own body, she was distracted and disturbed.

She spent her whole time with God this morning digging into His Word to find the way to freedom and found what she was looking for in, of all places, Ecclesiastes 3. "There is a time to die." Immediately the Holy Spirit began to inspire her to research what the Bible means when it says we are to "die to self." She had never really understood it when she had read that phrase before. But as the Spirit led her study, her heart began to burn with conviction. She didn't need to *mend* the obsession with her looks and her body image. Those old thought patterns needed to *die*.

It would require a trip to the Cross of Jesus in her time of prayer as she came to the end of her ability to fight the constant battle of low self-image. She surrendered herself completely, once again, to the work of Jesus in her heart. Today, she chose to die to self-centered, self-absorbed patterns of thinking concerning her body and to ask Jesus to replace her old thoughts with His. When she arose from several hours in prayer on her knees, she was a new person and ready to face the women at the convention with a new heart.

Read Ecclesiastes 3:1-3a.
¹For everything there is a season, and a time for every matter under heaven: ²a time to be born, and a time to die; a time to plant, and a time to pluck up what is planted; ³a time to kill, and a time to heal.

What do you think might need to be "killed" in this season of your life?

What needs to heal in this season of your life?

Read Galatians 2:20.
I have been crucified with Christ. It is no longer I who live, but Christ who lives in me. And the life I now live in the flesh I live by faith in the Son of God, who loved me and gave himself for me.

❋ What does it mean to be crucified with Christ?

Whether you are in the Winter Season due to your age or to circumstances, it is now time to rid your life of "flesh," which means having "self" in the center of your life. While this sounds contrary to popular opinion and our culture, it is the only way to joy and freedom in life, especially in a Winter Season. This is why Solomon got in trouble and landed in a dark place. He had turned from following the one true God and gave in to his fleshly desires. This departure from true worship led him to depression and self-absorption.

Our culture teaches us that the empty nest and retirement is "me time." It's the time to finally get to do what you want, when you want, the way you want and where you want to be. While it's true that first-world retirees have a lot of freedom of choice—and that's not a bad thing—as believers in Jesus Christ who have given our lives to Him, we will not find joy and true freedom by living self-centered lives. In every stage of life, self-centeredness and self-indulgence destroy relationships, damage our bodies, and shrivel our spirits. The pathway to the joy and freedom we all seek is in laying down our lives to serve Christ and those He's called us to love.

Read Romans 8:12-14.
12So then, brothers, we are debtors, not to the flesh, to live according to the flesh. 13For if you live according to the flesh you will die, but if by the Spirit you put to death the deeds of the body, you will live. 14For all who are led by the Spirit of God are sons of God.

According to verse 13, if you live according to your fleshy desires, what will happen? What kind of death occurs?

Fill in the blank from the scripture above:

"but if by the Spirit you_____

_____, you will live."

The wonderful thing about the Winter Season is that it's a time of reflection, whether you're here because you're in a pandemic, you're retired, you're not well, or you're in a crisis. It is a time at the crossroads of life where you can leave behind the parts of your life that need to be let go of and move forward into a new page of your life story. You don't want to drag into your new season old bitterness, unforgiveness, damaged relationships, hurts and wounds from injustice done to you and your loved ones. You don't want to try to move forward with old self-destructive habits. You don't even want to be engulfed in grief for the rest of your life. This is the time to close the chapter on the past and move into your future with hope.

This is the time to "kill" the flesh patterns that have enslaved you—whether it is being stuck in negative attitudes, destructive patterns of thinking, or any number of things that need to GO! Life is too short to spend it in self-destruction. It's time to ask God to clean up our act.

Lord Jesus, set me free from those things that bind me and keep me from living in the freedom, joy, and victory You bought for me with Your blood. Lord, I surrender my life to You. Forgive my sins and break every chain that keeps me in bondage, casting down all my wrong thinking and every proud and lofty thing in my life that exalts itself against the true knowledge of God. Bring into captivity my every thought to the obedience of Jesus, Messiah, the son of God. In Jesus' name I pray. Amen.

A Bit of Wisdom

When my mother was already past 90, she and I were talking very early one morning as we often did when I visited her. She was sharing some of her struggles in losing the companionship of my father who had advanced memory loss. I said, "Mama, let's pray together." And for the first time in my life, she said, "I just can't. You have to do it for me. I'm passed it!" My mom was out of the kind of spiritual energy and strength needed for intense battles in prayer. Before you "get passed it" and no longer have the energy for doing your spiritual homework, take the time now to wage war in prayer for God's kingdom to come in your situation.

Time to Heal — Day 5

Lord, I bring my body, my mind, and my heart before Your throne. Heal my every wound physically, emotionally and spiritually. I trust You with my physical needs while I walk this earth. Father, I also bring my heart and mind to You for healing. Pour the oil of the Holy Spirit on my deepest hurts. Give me the grace to forgive those who have sinned against me. I release them into Your hands and trust You to do what is best for them. You are Jehovah Rapha who heals me. I come to You. In Jesus' name I pray. Amen.

ELIZABETH WAS NEVER STRONG, but now something awful had taken hold of her body. It started with a butterfly-shaped rash across the bridge of her nose and across her cheeks. She thought it was a little sunburn. But soon afterwards, her shoulder and hip joints began to ache with an intensity that wasn't just exercise-induced. Then she started running fever. As a widow, her means were limited, so she didn't go to a doctor at first. She thought it was the flu, but after four continuous weeks of fever and aching, with no relief, she knew something was really wrong. Her first thought was cancer. How was it possible it was happening to her? It seemed too much to bear, and she was too sick right now to care. When Daphne stopped by for a visit, she found her beloved sister in a bad state. She immediately packed her in the car and headed for the emergency room. After days of tests and no improvement in Elizabeth's symptoms, the diagnosis came: lupus.

Cortisone and ibuprofen helped some, but every day it was a challenge just to move and to breathe. She began taking weekly injections of a newly approved medication said to make a difference. It did for a while, but the effects seemed to be wearing off.

Elizabeth's faith was tested to the core. But along this painful journey of suffering, she learned an amazing lesson that set her free. Her body was not free of pain, not free of the fevers, not free of aches and pains and overwhelming fatigue, but her heart and spirit were set free when she began to apply all she'd learned from the Lord about trusting Him and really letting go. Instead of begging for physical healing and seeking God just to get out of the painful assignment, she decided to take a leap of faith and entrust her broken body into His care, letting go of her self-effort and desires for physical, earthly healing. She knew He would heal her body if that was best in His eternal plan. But she also knew sometimes He withheld physical healing for a greater spiritual purpose. That's what she wanted: to see His kingdom come, His will to be done, no matter what came. She read again the familiar story of Jesus in Gethsemane from Matthew 26.

Read Matthew 26:36-42.

³⁶Then Jesus went with them to a place called Gethsemane, and he said to his disciples, "Sit here, while I go over there and pray." ³⁷And taking with him Peter and the two sons of Zebedee, he began to be sorrowful and troubled. ³⁸Then he said to them, "My soul is very sorrowful, even to death; remain here, and watch with me." ³⁹And going a little farther he fell on his face and prayed, saying, "My Father, if it be possible, let this cup pass from me; nevertheless, not as I will, but as you will." ⁴⁰And he came to the disciples and found them sleeping. And he said to Peter, "So, could you not watch with me one hour? ⁴¹Watch and pray that you may not enter into temptation. The spirit indeed is willing, but the flesh is weak." ⁴²Again, for the second time, he went away and prayed, "My Father, if this cannot pass unless I drink it, your will be done."

❋ What was Jesus' prayer the first time He prayed?

❋ What was Jesus' prayer the second time He prayed?

According to this passage, was this situation easy or hard for Jesus?

Which verses tell you how he felt?

Read Ecclesiastes 3:3a.
…and a time to heal…

Honestly, I was hesitant to approach the subject of "healing" when it came time to take down the "book" from the library of life called "a time to heal." I had two reasons. Actually, I made two excuses. First, the subject of healing among believers can be very controversial and touchy. It can be a test of faith and become grounds for serious arguments, and I just didn't want to go there. Secondly, one of our daughters has suffered from a chronic illness. My heart is very sensitive, as we have fasted and prayed, she has sought expert medical advice and followed it, and we have waited on God's healing. While we have seen some progress, we are still in the waiting room for her total healing.

And I had already written the first draft of this chapter when I tested positive for the Covid-19 virus. I couldn't believe it had happened to me. I had been so careful with physical distancing by remaining six feet from others, wearing masks and gloves and staying home most of the time. But it did happen at a small family gathering. It triggered my lifelong asthma, and breathing became my daily goal. But with much prayer, good medications, and David's tender, loving care, I was healed.

Then, 116 days later, I tested positive a second time for the Covid virus just as we were finishing the final edits of the book you are reading! The symptoms, the isolation, and the quarantine started all over again. It was hard not to feel discouraged. I thank the Lord that He brought me through the illness. We live in a fallen world where sickness can happen to anyone and we need the healing touch of Jesus.

Jesus cares about our physical suffering. We see His heart for the sick in Matthew 4:23.

*And he went throughout all Galilee, teaching in their synagogues and proclaiming the gospel of the kingdom and **healing** every disease and every affliction among the people.*

Read Luke 9:11.

*When the crowds learned it, they followed him, and he welcomed them and spoke to them of the kingdom of God and cured those who had need of **healing**.*

What were the main components of Jesus' ministry on earth according to Mathew 4:23?

Jesus had great compassion for the sick—those who suffered physically and those who were blind spiritually. We see Him teaching, preaching, and healing the sick everywhere He went during His earthly ministry, and His disciples learned to do the same.

Read the story of the healing of the lame man in Acts 3:2-16.
²And a man lame from birth was being carried, whom they laid daily at the gate of the temple that is called the Beautiful Gate to ask alms of those entering the temple. ³Seeing Peter and John about to go into the temple, he asked to receive alms. ⁴And Peter directed his gaze at him, as did John, and said, "Look at us." ⁵And he fixed his attention on them, expecting to receive something from them. ⁶But Peter said, "I have no silver and gold, but what I do have I give to you. In the name of Jesus Christ of Nazareth, rise up and walk!" ⁷And he took him by the right hand and raised him up, and immediately his feet and ankles were made strong. ⁸And leaping up, he stood and began to walk, and entered the temple with them, walking and leaping and praising God. ⁹And all the people saw him walking and praising God, ¹⁰and recognized him as the one who sat at the Beautiful Gate of the temple, asking for alms. And they were filled with wonder and amazement at what had happened to him.

Peter Speaks in Solomon's Portico

¹¹While he clung to Peter and John, all the people, utterly astounded, ran together to them in the portico called Solomon's. ¹²And when Peter saw it he addressed the people: "Men of Israel, why do you wonder at this, or why do you stare at us, as though by our own power or piety we have made him walk? ¹³The God of Abraham, the God of Isaac, and the God of Jacob, the God of our fathers, glorified his servant Jesus, whom you delivered over and denied in the presence of Pilate, when he had decided to release him. ¹⁴But you denied the Holy and Righteous One, and asked for a murderer to be granted to you, ¹⁵and you killed the Author of life, whom God raised from the dead. To this we are witnesses. ¹⁶And his name—by faith in his name—has made this man strong whom you see and know, and the faith that is through Jesus has given the man this perfect health in the presence of you all.

How did Peter facilitate the healing of the lame man?

Where did Peter explain the healing to those who witnessed the lame man's recovery?

Why is that location interesting from what you know about Solomon?

What is the most impressive thing to you in this story?

There IS a time to heal. God's time. Sometimes there are miraculous physical healings, as we read about it in the stories of Jesus and His disciples in Scripture. And we all know stories where this is true even today. We are told to ask, seek and knock, praying for God to bring restoration to broken bodies. But we must be careful not to order God to do our will. We must be cautious about accusing others of being faithless, and therefore remaining ill. We lay our requests at the feet of Jesus, have faith to believe He hears our prayers, obey His instructions and guidance about treatments, and trust it all into His care. We join the Psalmist in praying Psalm 27:14 *"Wait for the Lord; be strong, and let your heart take courage; wait for the Lord!"* And with Jesus in praying, *"Thy kingdom come, Thy will be done."*

Healing comes in many forms. Sometimes, healing comes emotionally when we allow old wounds to come to the surface, face them squarely, head-on, and then bring them to the feet of Jesus. If you will go back to that time and place where the hurt began, then see Him with you there, holding your hand, carrying the pain, you can entrust your deepest sorrows to Him. He is able to heal us from the inside out. As we forgive ourselves and forgive those who have sinned against us, our souls are set free and healing begins.

If your Winter Season began with an illness that won't go away, you may or may not find physical healing in your time left on earth, but you can have spiritual and emotional healing. While your body may not be responding to treatment and the outlook isn't what you planned, there is still "a time for healing" for you. This is the time to do two things: first, to grieve what you have lost. For you it might be mobility and flexibility. It might be being able to get out of bed and dress yourself or go where you want to go, when you want to go there. You might feel trapped in a body that won't cooperate. Instead of being angry and frustrated, it's time to take the second step when physical healing is needed. Go deeper into your relationship with Christ. Tell Him your sorrows, your grief, and your pain. Cry out to Him and cling to Him. Allow His love to invade your heart and soul. Open yourself to Jesus' overwhelming love and grace as you read this passage from Romans 8:15-38.

Read Romans 8:15-38.

15For you did not receive the spirit of slavery to fall back into fear, but you have received the Spirit of adoption as sons, by whom we cry, "Abba! Father!" 16The Spirit himself bears witness with our spirit that we are children of God, 17and if children, then heirs—heirs of God and fellow heirs with Christ, provided we suffer with him in order that we may also be glorified with him.

18For I consider that the sufferings of this present time are not worth comparing with the glory that is to be revealed to us. 19For the creation waits with eager longing for the revealing of the sons of God. 20For the creation was subjected to futility, not willingly, but because of him who subjected it, in hope 21that the creation itself will be set free from its bondage to corruption and obtain the freedom of the glory of the children of God. 22For we know that the whole creation has been groaning together in the pains of childbirth until now. 23And not only the creation, but we ourselves, who have the firstfruits of the Spirit, groan inwardly as we wait eagerly for adoption as sons, the redemption of our bodies. 24For in this hope we were saved. Now hope that is seen is not hope. For who hopes for what he sees? 25But if we hope for what we do not see, we wait for it with patience.

26Likewise the Spirit helps us in our weakness. For we do not know what to pray for as we ought, but the Spirit himself intercedes for us with groanings too deep for words. 27And he who searches hearts knows what is the mind of the Spirit, because the Spirit intercedes for the saints according to the will of God. 28And we know that for those who love God all things work together for good, for those who are called according to his purpose. 29For those whom he foreknew he also predestined to be conformed to the image of his Son, in order that he might be the firstborn among many brothers. 30And those whom he predestined he also called, and those whom he called he also justified, and those whom he justified he also glorified.

31What then shall we say to these things? If God is for us, who can be against us? 32He who did not spare his own Son but gave him up for us all, how will he not also with him graciously give us all things? 33Who shall bring any charge against God's elect? It is God who justifies.

³⁴Who is to condemn? Christ Jesus is the one who died—more than that, who was raised—who is at the right hand of God, who indeed is interceding for us. ³⁵Who shall separate us from the love of Christ? Shall tribulation, or distress, or persecution, or famine, or nakedness, or danger, or sword? ³⁶As it is written, "For your sake we are being killed all the day long; we are regarded as sheep to be slaughtered." ³⁷No, in all these things we are more than conquerors through him who loved us. ³⁸For I am sure that neither death nor life, nor angels nor rulers, nor things present nor things to come, nor powers, ³⁹nor height nor depth, nor anything else in all creation, will be able to separate us from the love of God in Christ Jesus our Lord.

A Bit of Wisdom

When it comes to healing, you have your part to play. No matter how old or young you are, you can contribute to your own health. Your body needs nutritious food, regular exercise, plenty of sleep, and less stress. Make some small, achievable goals for your overall health and celebrate each small accomplishment. Today there are watches and apps that can make it easy to track your progress.

If and when you do get sick or have an accident, call for help. It may be hard for you, but don't hesitate to reach out for medical assistance when needed.

WEEK 4
WHAT TIME IS IT?
PART 2

A Personal Message to You from Solomon

As you navigate the good times and the bad ones, you will choose how to travel through them. You can see the glass half-full or half-empty. Do yourself and everyone around you a big favor. Choose joy no matter what your circumstance is right now. In the middle of your struggle, you can find moments, and maybe even a season of joy, hope, and laughter. The choice is yours.

A Time to Weep, and a Time to Laugh

Day 1

Lord, give me the grace I need to know when it is time to weep and mourn and when it is time to laugh and dance. Lord Jesus, sometimes I get stuck in despair and depression and have a hard time laughing and having fun. I choose today to fix my eyes on You, plant my feet on You, my rock, and I choose joy. I love you, Lord. In Jesus' name I pray, Amen.

THE SISTERS learned that communication with each other through the Winter Season would carry them through the heartache of losing their beloved parents and weathering the storms of Elizabeth's illness and Daphne's divorce. They kept up the group chat they had established on their phones to be able to send quick texts throughout the day. Most of the messages were written prayers and prayer requests. Some were about serious decisions they needed to make or actions that needed to be put in place to close their parents' estate. But sometimes, they shared the funny things the grandkids said or a happy memory triggered by something no one else would understand. They sent old pictures to each other from their childhood, and the shared laughter and tears carried them as they journeyed through the Winter Season.

Read Ecclesiastes 3:1-4.

¹For everything there is a season, and a time for every matter under heaven: ²a time to be born, and a time to die; a time to plant, and a time to pluck up what is planted; ³a time to kill, and a time to heal; a time to break down, and a time to build up; ⁴a time to weep, and a time to laugh; a time to mourn, and a time to dance;

❋ Which of the seasons listed are your choice and which are up to the sovereignty of God?

When in your life has there been a time to weep and mourn?

❋ When in your life has there been a time to laugh and dance?

Solomon reminds us that God is in control of the seasons of our lives. We don't choose the day of our birth, nor the time of our death. Events out of our control happen to all of us that cause grief or joy. God is a sovereign God, and He is in control. When we fight for control, we always lose. When we surrender to Him, releasing our grip on trying to manipulate and control our "seasons," we will experience joy and peace. If we are wise as we age, we will learn to "go with the flow." Life will bring change and if we embrace our current season, seeking God's will and following His heart, we will find that He is able to take us by the hand and carry us through each era of our lives victoriously. While some seasons of life are more difficult than others, His grace is sufficient for each one.

Even though you acknowledge the sovereignty of God and are in His will, you are still human and you will experience the emotions of each season. Part of the difficulty of the Winter Season is the emotional roller coaster that will take you for a ride. Winter Season is full of transitions and changes, some of them unwelcomed; and, for many people, this brings on emotions you didn't even know you had. You'll care about things you never dreamed you would care about. You might become sentimental about the silliest thing. You may cry over a triggered memory and laugh when others might think it inappropriate. It's okay to experience your experiences. You need to feel what you feel. Allow yourself to cry when you need a good cry and, at every opportunity, laugh until the tears roll.

When we are under the heavy burden of care-giving, we need to find ways to do something so enjoyable that it brings a smile. When we go through a tough circumstance that brings with it emotional pain, we need the balance of levity, joy, and laughter. When we go through the death of a loved one, sometimes we feel guilty for being happy, even for a moment. But our hearts need a break when we're sad and grieving. The laughter doesn't negate the tears nor the memories, and laughter really is the best medicine.

Read and fill in the blanks from Proverbs 17:22.

A joyful heart is good medicine, but a crushed spirit dries up the bones. A_____ heart is good medicine, but a _____ _____ dries up the bones.

The Bible is full of stories of people going through a Winter Season. In the Old Testament, the book of Jeremiah tells the story of Jeremiah, the prophet, exhorting the Israelites over and over to return to faith in God...or suffer the consequences. The people didn't listen, and their Winter Season began when God allowed the Babylonians to carry out His judgment by destroying their cities and carrying off captives. But Winter Seasons don't last forever! Despite the Israelites' disobedience, God promised to rescue His people and return them home after 70 years.

Read Jeremiah 31:10-13.
¹⁰"Hear the word of the LORD, O nations, and declare it in the coastlands far away; say, 'He who scattered Israel will gather him, and will keep him as a shepherd keeps his flock.'¹¹For the LORD has ransomed Jacob and has redeemed him from hands too strong for him.¹²They shall come and sing aloud on the height of Zion, and they shall be radiant over the goodness of the LORD, over the grain, the wine, and the oil, and over the young of the flock and the herd; their life shall be like a watered garden, and they shall languish no more.¹³Then shall the young women rejoice in the dance, and the young men and the old shall be merry. I will turn their mourning into joy; I will comfort them, and give them gladness for sorrow.

What does the Lord do for His people in verse 10?

Fill in the blanks in verse 11:

For the LORD has _____ Jacob and has _____ him from hands too strong for him.

✸ How has the Lord been your Shepherd?

How did the people of Israel celebrate God's loving care for them?

✸ What can you do this week, even if on a very small scale, to do what the children of Israel did?

It's easy to get down emotionally because sometimes your "feeler" gets stuck in the down mode and won't return easily to joy. This is when music can lift your spirits and bring you back into balance. Listening to a whole playlist of uplifting worship music can completely change your mood. When I was deep in grief and stress over my parents' deaths and my daughter's health, sometimes my quiet time alone with God would consist of listening to a whole worship album. Worship music brought the calm and peace I needed.

King David was a person in the Bible who knew a lot about the Winter Season. Although God had anointed him the next king of Israel after Saul, that change in authority was a long time coming. David spent years on the run for his life while King Saul continued to hunt him down, seeking to destroy him. You can read in many chapters in Psalms about his Winter Season where he felt afraid and abandoned while his enemies pursued him. But just as Solomon notes in Ecclesiastes 3:1-4, the time for weeping and mourning will come to an end, and the time for dancing and laughter will arrive. For David, his Winter Season came to an end when he was finally crowned king of Israel and the ark of the covenant returned to Jerusalem.

Read II Samuel 6:12b-16, 20-23.

¹²...*So, David went and brought up the ark of God from the house of Obed-edom to the city of David with rejoicing.* ¹³*And when those who bore the ark of the LORD had gone six steps, he sacrificed an ox and a fattened animal.* ¹⁴*And David danced before the LORD with all his might. And David was wearing a linen ephod.* ¹⁵*So David and all the house of Israel brought up the ark of the LORD with shouting and with the sound of the horn.*

¹⁶*As the ark of the LORD came into the city of David, Michal the daughter of Saul looked out of the window and saw King David leaping and dancing before the LORD, and she despised him in her heart.*

²⁰*And David returned to bless his household. But Michal the daughter of Saul came out to meet David and said, "How the king of Israel honored himself today, uncovering himself today before the eyes of his servants' female servants, as one of the vulgar fellows shamelessly uncovers himself!"* ²¹*And David said to Michal, "It was before the LORD, who chose me above your father and above all his house, to appoint me as prince over Israel, the people of the LORD—and I will celebrate before the LORD.* ²²*I will make myself yet more contemptible than this, and I will be abased in your eyes. But by the female servants of whom you have spoken, by them I shall be held in honor."* ²³*And Michal the daughter of Saul had no child to the day of her death.*

Finish this phrase from verses 14 and 16:
¹⁴*And David* _____ _____ _____ _____ *with all his might.*

¹⁶*Michal the daughter of Saul looked out of the window and saw King David* _____ *and* _____ *before the Lord and she* _____ *him in her heart.*

✸ Why was it appropriate for David to dance?

❋ Why did Michal, his wife, despise David at this time?

God was pouring out blessings on King David, and it was time to come out of the dark time with great rejoicing, but his joy was not shared by his wife, Michal, the daughter of Saul. She didn't want David to embarrass her with his public, emotional display, even if it was in the act of worshiping God. The Bible tells us she "despised" him for dancing with joy in public.

Others might not understand our laughter in the middle of a difficult situation. But if you can manage it, the healthiest thing to do when you are under a heavy load is to lighten that load with God's gift of laughter. God gave us joy to enjoy! It's a good thing to leap and dance before the Lord with all of your might, especially after a long Winter Season.

Read Psalm 30 where David writes...
⁴Sing praises to the LORD, O you his saints, and give thanks to his holy name. ⁵For his anger is but for a moment, and his favor is for a lifetime. Weeping may tarry for the night, but joy comes with the morning.

A Bit of Wisdom

Sometimes you just have to laugh at yourself. One Thanksgiving, I had cooked for three days to make all the preparations for our family feast. The tables were set in my best linens and china, and all was ready as our children and grandchildren arrived. I sent two of our sons-in-law on a special errand close by. I had ordered the turkey that year from a very special place, and it was ready right at that moment to be collected and brought into the house. We were laughing and talking over the appetizers when the two young men walked in the door with ashen faces. They told me that the turkeys (I needed two!) were FROZEN! I am used to unmerciful teasing at the hands of my beloved sons-in-law, so I said, "Right! Just put the turkeys here on the platters." The guys assured me that indeed the turkeys were like frozen rocks. I had unknowingly ordered the pre-cooked but frozen turkeys that should have been thawing in the refrigerator for several days!

I had a choice in that moment to dissolve in tears and hysteria or start laughing. I'm a bit proud to say I chose the latter. That year we had a vegetarian Thanksgiving, and it was delicious. We barely missed the turkey among the dishes piled up with all the trimmings. Over the many desserts on the table, we declared it to be the best Thanksgiving ever!

Casting Down and Gathering Stones

Day 2

Lord Jesus, I want to walk in step with Your Spirit. I ask You to direct my steps and order my priorities, teaching me more about the season in which I now live. Open the eyes of my heart and flood them with light. Help me to let go of the past and take hold of future promises and possibilities. I bind my mind to Your mind and my heart to Your heart. Loose and destroy wrong thinking patterns in me and wrong attitudes, especially about my circumstances right now. Lord, I choose to believe You, to live and have my being in You, and to focus on Your face, even and especially when it's hard not to be discouraged. You are my Rock and my Redeemer. Bless the name of the Lord. Amen.

Madeline had lived in Asia now for a decade and was comfortable speaking the language and negotiating what were, for her, strange cultural norms. She was a woman of mighty faith, and she knew that God was in control of her life and that of her family; but living in a country with an unstable government and radicalized groups who were terrorizing foreigners, was unnerving. She couldn't shake the nagging fears that sometimes kept her up at night.

It had started when she was just a little girl. She was afraid of the dark, afraid of being alone and could never watch a scary movie. As she grew older, those fears took a different turn. Fear had begun to rule her heart and influence her decisions. Living in a different country and culture just fed the irrational fears that plagued her. One night, she finally cried out to God for help to bring down the pattern of fearfulness that consumed her.

Read Ecclesiastes 3:1, 5.
¹For everything there is a season, and a time for every matter under heaven…
⁵a time to cast away stones, and a time to gather stones together.

What are the opposing actions on the stones?

While Solomon could have been referring to gathering stones for boundary walls or casting out stones in a field to prepare for planting, he doesn't specify which stones he was talking about. He wisely leaves it open to our own interpretation. The direction God led me as I meditated on the stones was to cast away stones and to gather stones concerning spiritual strongholds. Historically, a stronghold is a place that has been fortified to protect it from attack. Think of it as a castle or fortress. A stronghold keeps something out and something else inside. The Bible speaks of strongholds in two opposing concepts. The first is that God is our stronghold.

Read II Samuel 22:3.
*³My God, my rock, in whom I take refuge, my shield, and the horn of my salvation, my **stronghold** and my refuge, my savior; you save me from violence.*

What does "stronghold" mean in this verse?

Draw a simple picture here to illustrate the verse above.

Read Psalm 9:9.
The LORD is a stronghold for the oppressed, a stronghold in times of trouble.

How would you write this verse in your own words as it applies to your life right now?

Read Psalm 27:1.
The Lord is my light and my salvation; whom shall I fear? The Lord is the stronghold of my life; of whom shall I be afraid?

Why can you trust God when you are afraid?

God is our defender and protector. We run to Him to take refuge. That is one kind of stronghold, where we are inside the "fortress," protected from evil and harm by God Almighty. Praying for and affirming God's protection over your life and that of your family is a time to gather stones together, creating a defense against the enemy.

You can gather stones around your children and grandchildren by praying for them. If you are retired from your full-time employment, you have flexible time schedules; and the best thing about that is that you have extended time to pray. David and I spend time each morning reading our Bibles, then with coffee and tea cups in hand, we "gather stones together" by praying a hedge of protection around our children and grandchildren and interceding for their needs. We pray for their spiritual, emotional, and physical protection. We pray for the blood of Jesus Christ to cover them. We hold up our shields of faith over them to reject the fiery darts of Satan, their enemy. We pray that all sinful strongholds in their hearts and minds be broken down and that God would do a mighty work in each one of their lives. We pray that they will be pillars in God's kingdom, movers and shakers to see His will be done on the earth through their surrendered lives. You cannot make choices for your children. You can't keep your grandchildren locked away from the world. But you can pray for them. And your prayers for them are powerful.

Read Ephesians 6:18.
…praying at all times in the Spirit, with all prayer and supplication. To that end, keep alert with all perseverance, making supplication for all the saints.

Read James 5:16 in the King James version of the Bible.
Confess your faults one to another, and pray one for another, that ye may be healed. The effectual fervent prayer of a righteous man availeth much.

What do these verses teach you about prayer?

How do you want to incorporate today's Scripture readings into your prayer life?

Solomon tells us there is a time to "gather stones" but also a time to "cast away stones." Casting away stones also has to do with "strongholds."

Read II Corinthians 10:3-5.
³For though we walk in the flesh, we are not waging war according to the flesh. ⁴For the weapons of our warfare are not of the flesh but have divine power to destroy strongholds. ⁵We destroy arguments and every lofty opinion raised against the knowledge of God, and take every thought captive to obey Christ.

✺ What can the weapons of our spiritual warfare accomplish?

✺ What are the three parts of our warfare against spiritual strongholds according to verse 5?

1.
2.
3.

If you have time, go to biblehub.com and click on the Strong's tab. Then type in II Corinthians 10:4, and you will discover the meaning behind the Greek word for "stronghold," which is *ochurόma* or in Greek ὀχύρωμα. It is pronounced "okh-oo'-ro-mah."

Write down what you learn.

___
___
___
___

Ochuróma or "stronghold" is a fortified, military strong-walled fortress. In II Corinthians 10:4, the word "stronghold" is used by Paul in a negative sense and "is used figuratively of a false argument in which a person seeks 'shelter' (a safe place) to escape reality."[1] This is a stronghold that needs to come down because it keeps the bad things in—like fear, pride, and anger—and the good things out—like love, joy, and peace.

Tearing down strongholds is work that we do in prayer. A stronghold is a pattern of wrong thoughts that take us in the wrong direction. This is what needs to be cast down and destroyed. And it only happens in fervent prayer with a surrendered heart ready for God's holy heart surgery.

If we have a habit of prideful thoughts and actions, then pride is a stronghold in our lives that keeps in wrong thinking and attitudes and keeps out truth and the light of Jesus. If fear drives our choices and decisions, we have a stronghold that cripples us and causes destruction in relationships and prevents us from having abundant life. A stronghold is more than one sinful action or thought. It is a habitual, deeply-ingrained false pattern of thinking that leads life down the wrong path.

How can we "cast away stones," breaking down a stronghold in our hearts? How do we get rid of these patterns of thinking and acting that have ruled and ruined our lives? This work can only be done by the Holy Spirit with your cooperation. The way to cooperate with the Spirit's work is to humbly submit the stronghold into His hands and allow Him to destroy it. The first step is to admit the stronghold exists—whether it is pride or fear, lust or greed, anger, unforgiveness, or passivity—and surrender it before the throne of God. Then, pray II Corinthians 10:4 something like this: *"Lord Jesus, I cast down all of my wrong and sinful patterns of thought in this area of my life, and every prideful, rebellious barrier wall that keeps me from obeying and honoring You in this part of my heart, and I bring my every thought captive to the obedience of Jesus, Messiah, the Son of God. Deliver me from this stronghold in Jesus' name and bring in Your holy light to fill my heart with Your life. I surrender all of this completely into Your hands. In the name of Jesus I pray, Amen."*

Read Galatians 2:20 as a prayer.
I have been crucified with Christ. It is no longer I who live, but Christ who lives in me. And the life I now live in the flesh I live by faith in the Son of God, who loved me and gave himself for me.

Who is crucified with Christ and what does that mean?

Dying to self, to sin, and to strongholds will set you free. Paul says he has been crucified with Christ. Our strongholds don't need *mending*; they need to be *crucified*. Jesus died on the cross to set us free from the chains of our strongholds. When we surrender them to Him, die to them, and cut off the power they have over us, we can live the abundant life promised to those who believe Jesus.

In the Winter Season, spend more time praying than ever before. The prayers you pray to tear down strongholds and to sow spirit-life into the lives around you will bear fruit. You may not live to see all that your prayers accomplish; but if you pray, you can rest assured you have done the most important work in partnership with God. And He will accomplish everything and more than you can imagine.

[1]*Strong's Exhaustive Concordance of the Bible,* Greek Number 3794.

A Bit of Wisdom

Here is an example of praying down strongholds:

"Lord, I worship only You. I choose to set my mind on the mind of Christ, and I am ready to take off my mask. I ask You today to cleanse my heart, demolishing and destroying all the strongholds in my mind that are hostile to the life of Christ Jesus living in me. Lord, please crush the wrong patterns of thought running in my mind that cause me to think, respond and react in wrong ways. I trust You, Lord, to do this work in me and for me. I know I cannot do this for myself, but I trust Your Holy Spirit to cleanse and renew my mind. I thank You, Lord Jesus, that You will complete the good work You have begun in me. I ask You to put a guard around my mind and heart, protecting my mind from attacks of the enemy.

Now, Lord, I pray for _____. I ask you to destroy the wrong thinking in _____'s mind, and to saturate _____'s mind with the Word of God filled with Your truth. I pray that the truth would set _____ free. Please destroy and demolish all wrong patterns of thinking in _____ that are hostile to You and to the truth. Lord, please station a guard around _____'s heart and mind, protecting him/her from the enemy. Lord, I ask You to break down all the resistance and rebellion that remains standing in _____'s heart, mind, and will. I pray that every barrier wall keeping the lies in and the Truth out of _____'s life would be completely demolished and destroyed.

Father, I ask You to take into captivity all the darkness in _____'s mind. I ask You to demolish all the wrong thought processes that have formed through traumatic emotional events and through old wrong-thinking patterns handed down through the generations.

I thank You that You are trustworthy. I place _____'s life into Your hands. I am asking for victory over all the darkness and for every lie to be exposed. Lord, please heal everything You choose to reveal. I pray for victory in this battle. I praise You, Lord. While I can't see what You are doing and often don't understand Your ways, I do trust You. I trust Your purposes and Your divine will. Do all that is in Your heart and in Your mind to do, Lord.

I thank You that You are doing a work in them much more than I can see. You are working to accomplish Your holy purposes and plans that You have for him/her to give them hope and a future. I entrust him/her into Your hands, Lord. In Jesus' name. Amen."

Embracing and Refraining

Day 3

Lord, thank You for loving me with agape, perfect love. Thank you also for giving me precious ones to receive my love. Jesus, please purify my motives so that my love is untainted and without manipulation. Pour Your love through me that I might be a channel of blessing. In Jesus' name I pray. Amen.

As the eldest sister, Abigail always mothered her siblings. Now, God had blessed her with her own tribe to cluck about, tucking them under her wings whenever possible. When her last baby was born, her firstborn was already in high school. With six children of her own, her life had consisted of almost nothing but mothering her brood. But now they were almost grown, and one by one they began to leave her carefully feathered nest. She wept over each parting as if she would never see them again. But the last one to leave, her baby, was the hardest of all.

This was the child of her heart. This boy was tender-hearted, even while maintaining his rugged masculinity. He was kind to all, but he loved his mama. And she loved him! Their relationship was more than mother and son; they were prayer partners and great friends. While her husband was a good and godly man, he didn't share her passion for prayer and had no patience with reading, studying and listening to sermons online. But this young man was hungry for the things of God, and she watched as God shaped him to be a mighty pillar in His kingdom. Now he was leaving home, and her heart was breaking. How could she let him go?

Read Ecclesiastes 3:1, 5b.
¹For everything there is a season, and a time for every matter under heaven: ⁵...a time to embrace, and a time to refrain from embracing;

Write the initials of a person in your life who needs your embrace.

_____

List some times a special embrace has made you feel loved.

Oxytocin is a chemical in our bodies that scientists sometimes call the "cuddle hormone." This is because its levels rise when we hug, touch, or sit close to someone else. Oxytocin is associated with happiness and less stress. Scientists have found that this hormone has a strong effect on women.[2] So hugging is a healthy thing to do.

Read I John 3:16-18.
¹⁶This is how we know what love is: Jesus Christ laid down his life for us. And we ought to lay down our lives for our brothers and sisters. ¹⁷If anyone has material possessions and sees a brother or sister in need but has no pity on them, how can the love of God be in that person? ¹⁸Dear children, let us not love with words or speech but with actions and in truth.

✺ What is a practical way to embrace someone who needs love?

If your Winter Season is one where you find yourself alone, find someone who needs your embrace. An elderly neighbor, a young mom, or a little child needing your love are usually right around you. Just open your eyes to whom God has placed in your path. Your pastor's wife might need encouragement and love on a personal level. Take her to lunch to express your appreciation and love. The more you pour out love, the more your own heart will feel full and satisfied. Reba McEntire sang a song in the early 1980's written by Don Roth and Timmy Tappan titled "Love Isn't Love Til You Give It Away." You'll find it on YouTube with a Google search. Here are the words:

> A smile's not a smile until it wrinkles your face,
> Bell's not a bell without ringing
> A home's not a home when there's nobody there
> A song's not a song without singing
>
> Love isn't love till you give it away
> Love isn't love till it's free
> The love in your heart
> Wasn't put there to stay
> Oh love isn't love till you give it away
>
> You might think love is a treasure to keep
> Feeling to cherish and hold
> But love is a treasure for people to share
> You keep it by letting it go
>
> Love isn't love till you give it away
> Love isn't love till it's free
> The love in your heart
> Wasn't put there to stay
> Oh love isn't love till you give it away

Cause love can't survive
When it's hidden inside
And love was meant to be shared

Love isn't love till you give it away
Love isn't love till it's free
The love in your heart
Wasn't put there to stay
Oh love isn't love till you give it away

And of course, there is intimate embracing within marriage.

Read I Corinthians 7:2-5.
²But since sexual immorality is occurring, each man should have sexual relations with his own wife, and each woman with her own husband. ³The husband should fulfill his marital duty to his wife, and likewise the wife to her husband. ⁴The wife does not have authority over her own body but yields it to her husband. In the same way, the husband does not have authority over his own body but yields it to his wife. ⁵Do not deprive each other except perhaps by mutual consent and for a time, so that you may devote yourselves to prayer. Then come together again so that Satan will not tempt you because of your lack of self-control.

When is it appropriate in marriage to embrace?

When is it appropriate to refrain from embracing your mate?

God gave sex to us as a gift to be enjoyed within a covenant marriage. It is the ultimate full embrace that satisfies our spirits and souls as well as our bodies when it is between two believers in Christ who are one in Him. The sexual relationship is so very precious, private, and personal. Take seriously pleasing your mate and building soul, as well as body oneness in your marriage.

If you are in the golden years of retirement when you have your mate by your side in good health with time to spend together, this is the time to fully embrace. Hold each other close and nurture your marriage. Long walks while holding hands, sitting close on the sofa at night, and lingering over dinner are some of the perks of this stage of life. Some couples find they struggle and fight more during this part of their Winter Season. Nerve endings are raw, bodies ache, adult children are in trouble, grandchildren make poor choices, and the news is depressing. There are always reasons you can find to be grumpy and short-tempered. I want to encourage you to lay aside little complaints and focus on loving and embracing the one to whom you pledged your life "in sickness and in health, so long as you both shall live." Find creative ways to rev up your sex life. Be thoughtful and kind throughout the day. Do the little things you know he loves the most. Compromise on what to watch on television. Turn on the music from your dating years. Make the golden years golden!

Solomon teaches us that there is also a time to refrain from embracing. We have all lived through an unprecedented time of refraining from embracing that has affected our whole lives. Until the early part of 2020, most of us had never heard of "social distancing." Why would we want to keep six feet from the nearest human? The coronavirus that swept through the world changed all of that. First reported on December 31, 2019, the world was engulfed in fear as news came of a virulent, devastating virus, leaving many very ill and some dead. The only real way to win the war against this invader was isolation to keep from spreading the disease. So, we all went into quarantine. Schools, restaurants, gyms, businesses, and even churches closed their doors. We learned to have virtual worship services where everyone gathered online. Children were homeschooled by harried parents, helping them get their lessons by email. We were encouraged to order take-out from local restaurants to keep them in business, while few customers could be seated inside.

At the beginning of the pandemic, grocery stores became the front line of the battle of fear and loss of control. The only time people were willing to forego social distancing was to fight through crowded grocery stores, grabbing rolls and rolls of toilet paper and antibacterial hand sanitizer. Hoarding supplies and food became a world-wide obsession. Neighbors and friends had to avoid each other. Grandparents were separated from beloved grandchildren for fear that the children would unknowingly spread the virus to the older generation who were known to be the most vulnerable in the crisis. We learned the hard way that there was definitely a time to refrain from embracing. Thankfully, this is not the norm.

However, refraining from embracing refers to more than just a pandemic. We will have to take down this "book" from the library of life from time to time. One of those times is when it is the season to launch a child and let them go. Letting go of our children, refraining from holding them too tightly, is one of the greatest challenges of good parenting. No doubt, for many of us, it is hard, but it is healthy to release our children and let them fly out of the nest. It is a natural and necessary step for every family.

If you've read my Bible study *Freedom for Mothers*, you know how God taught me to let go of my eldest daughter as she was growing up and moving out of the house. He took me to Ecclesiastes 3 and instructed me to "refrain from embracing" her for a season to help her move into adulthood. Sometimes the most loving thing you can do is to let go.

Write the initials of a person in your life who needs for you to refrain from embracing. _____

You might have easily come up with the initials of a person who needs your tender love and a warm hug. But thinking of who needs for you to step back and refrain from embracing might have been harder. Love is the gift God gave to the world, and it is our joy and privilege to allow Him to pour His love through us, but we need wisdom to know how and when to draw others in and when to let them go.

[2]"What Are the Benefits of Hugging?" 11 April 2018, healthline.com.

A Bit of Wisdom

• In your marriage, how can you fully embrace your mate, emotionally and physically? What do you need to start doing or stop doing to take them into your heart and into your arms?

• If you are single, which of your friends needs a visit and a good hug?

• With your adult children, how can you embrace them right now in a way they will experience your love? How should you refrain from embracing and smothering them with controlling attitudes?

• When your adult child brings home a potential mate, you will probably be faced with conflicting emotions. Are they the right one for your child? Is this the right time for marriage? Can you accept your child's choice? In our experience, embracing and accepting your child's choice of a mate is usually the right road. There are exceptions, of course, if the relationship is toxic, but most of the time, if you will embrace this new person into your heart and into your family, you will lay the foundation for a good relationship for the long haul. If you have raised your child to love the Lord and they are following His will, you can trust them.

On the other hand, if you hold back your love and acceptance, your child and their mate will sense your reluctance and you might pay for that decision for many years to come. Remember, at every holiday, this person will probably treat you the way you treated them in those early days!

• Grandchildren are so loveable, it usually is easy to embrace them. Do you need to work on spending more time with them? How can you embrace and bond with them in a healthy way that is encouraging? Is there a time or way you need to refrain from holding them too tightly to give their parents a rightful place in their life?

Time to Manage the Money

Day 4

Lord, thank You for providing all that I need. You have been so good to me and my family. Forgive me for distrusting You and Your heart for me and for complaining about what I lack. Father, today, I put my trust in You alone with all of my finances. Show me the way to obey Your instructions about managing our money. I love You, Lord, and thank You for caring for me. In Jesus' name. Amen.

DAPHNE struggled to make ends meet. After the divorce, she worked hard but earned little. Providing for the kids to go to university was really hard, but she had found a way through scholarships, grants and loans to get them through. The kids had found good jobs, so she didn't worry about them any more. She'd been trying to put aside money for her own elder care, not to burden them, but now most of what she had painstakingly saved was gone. She had no control over the swings of the stock market and the national financial situation. She needed God's wisdom to manage her money.

Read Ecclesiastes 3:1, 6.
¹*For everything there is a season, and a time for every matter under heaven:* ⁶ᵃ*time to seek, and a time to lose; a time to keep, and a time to cast away.*

Applying this passage to handling your money, what are some important milestones of managing your finances that you have already accomplished? What do you need to work on now?

Week 4: Day 4

Renowned commentator Matthew Henry, a Welsh minister from the late 1600s, wrote about the time to "seek," "lose," "keep," and "cast away:"

> [To seek] is a time to "get money, get preferment, get good bargains and a good interest, when opportunity smiles, a time when a wise man will seek (so the word is); when he is setting out in the world and has a growing family, when he is in his prime, when he prospers and has a run of business, then it is time for him to be busy and make hay when the sun shines. There is a time to get wisdom, and knowledge, and grace, when a man has a price put into his hand; but then let him expect there will come a time to spend, when all he has will be little enough to serve his turn. Nay, there will come a time to lose, when what has been soon got will be soon scattered and cannot be held fast. 9. A time to keep, when we have use for what we have got, and can keep it without running the hazard of a good conscience; but there may come a time to cast away, when love to God may oblige us to cast away what we have, because we must deny Christ and wrong our consciences if we keep it (Matt. 10:37, 38), and rather to make shipwreck of all than of the faith; nay, when love to ourselves may oblige us to cast it away, when it is for the saving of our lives, as it was when Jonah's mariners heaved their cargo into the sea."[3]

Name the top five of your possessions that are most important to you to keep for the present and future?

1.

2.

3.

4.

5.

Which of your things should you cast away?

1.

2.

3.

4.

5.

Financial management is one of those things that comes with living on planet earth. We are all entrusted with caring for financial resources, whether large or small. There is a time to seek and build your financial base with hard work, good money management, and careful savings. And there is a time in most of our lives where money is scarce, and it's a season to manage with less. There is a time to keep what we have, saving carefully for the future and a time to "cast it away," spending on something important.

Finances are fickle and easily come, then quickly go without warning. The stock market rises and falls with the political climate, with the weather changes, and with the whims of investors. How we handle wealth is one clear measure of our hearts. Solomon teaches us throughout his writings how to wisely handle the financial resources God has given to us.

Read Proverbs 3:9, 10.
⁹Honor the Lord with your wealth and with the firstfruits of all your produce; ¹⁰then your barns will be filled with plenty, and your vats will be bursting with wine.

What principle of money management do you find in this verse?

Read Proverbs 11:24.
²⁴One gives freely, yet grows all the richer; another withholds what he should give, and only suffers want.

What principle of money management do you find in this verse?

Read Proverbs 12:27.
Whoever is slothful will not roast his game, but the diligent man will get precious wealth.

What principle of money management do you find in this verse?

Read Proverbs 13:11.
Wealth gained hastily will dwindle, but whoever gathers little by little will increase it.

What principle of money management do you find in this verse?

Read Psalm 62:9, 10.
⁹Those of low estate are but a breath; those of high estate are a delusion; in the balances they go up; they are together lighter than a breath. ¹⁰Put no trust in extortion; set no vain hopes on robbery; if riches increase, set not your heart on them.

What principle of money management do you find in this verse?

Let's review basic biblical principles of managing our wealth from the verses above: We are to give to God and His kingdom first, we are to be generous with all that we have, we need to work hard and not be lazy, we aren't to enter into "get rich quick" schemes but to increase wealth little by little, and we're not to trust in riches but only in God.

Financial security is a big concern for most of us, but Jesus gives us some needed advice and encouragement.

Read Matthew 6: 31-34.

³¹Therefore do not be anxious, saying, 'What shall we eat?' or 'What shall we drink?' or 'What shall we wear?' ³²For the Gentiles seek after all these things, and your heavenly Father knows that you need them all. ³³But seek first the kingdom of God and his righteousness, and all these things will be added to you. ³⁴Therefore do not be anxious about tomorrow, for tomorrow will be anxious for itself. Sufficient for the day is its own trouble.

✺ Write out a prayer incorporating the Scripture above. You don't need to use all of the passage, but choose the lines and phrases that resonate in your heart.

I pray the Lord sets you free of worrying about your finances through the truth of His Word and the instruction of the Holy Spirit as you lean into Him, trusting Him to provide all your needs according to His riches in Christ Jesus. As you learn to manage the resources God has entrusted to you, "trust in the Lord with all your heart and lean not to your own understanding. In all your ways acknowledge Him, and He will direct your paths." (Proverbs 3:5, 6).

³*Commentary on the Whole Bible* by Matthew Henry, p. 795.

A Bit of Wisdom

If you are struggling with spending more than your means, use a simple budget to get back on track. Dave Ramsey's ministry (daveramsey.com) has excellent tools to help you harness your resources and move into financial freedom.

A Time for Relationship

Lord, You are King of kings and Lord of lords, and I bow before You today. Lord Jesus, I bring my relationships before You and ask that You would give me insight and wisdom for each one. I pray that You would lead me, guide me, instruct me in how to love unconditionally and, at the same time, have healthy boundaries. Fill me with Your Holy Spirit. I love You and commit my life and my family into Your hands. In Jesus' name, Amen.

CELINA was the middle child of the Page family in every way imaginable. When they were growing up, she was the go-between in arguments between the sisters and was everyone's best friend. They confided in her, sought counsel from her, and knew she was genuinely interested and concerned for each one. Even now that the sisters were all mature adults, she was the person everyone in the family consulted for relationship advice. Besides, she was fun to talk to. Celina laughed easily and could find joy on the darkest day.

But today, she faced a challenge. Her daughter, Amber, was having trouble with her mother-in-law; and Celina was at a loss as to how to help her. She prayed for wisdom to guide her daughter in how to have a healthy relationship with the woman who would someday be the "other" grandmother. Over a cup of coffee, Celina and Amber discussed what Celina was learning from Solomon about relationships. "It's all about timing. There's a time to speak and a time to keep your mouth closed. There's a time to bond and a time to give the relationship some space. Let's ask the Lord what time it is in this relationship."

Read Ecclesiastes 3: 1, 7, 8.
¹For everything there is a season, and a time for every matter under heaven: ⁷a time to tear, and a time to sew; a time to keep silence, and a time to speak; ⁸a time to love, and a time to hate; a time for war, and a time for peace.

Apply each of these "times" to relationships in your life and write the initials of the person it relates to in this season.

A time to tear-

A time to sew-

A time to keep silence-

A time to speak-

A time to love-

A time to "hate"-

A time for war-

A time to peace -

There is a time to "tear" our garments when we are in grief and a time to "sew" them again when the grief is over. There is a time to tear ourselves away from a relationship that is toxic for us and a time to mend a relationship and come close together again. And there is a time to keep silent.

Read Psalm 4:4.
Be angry, and do not sin; ponder in your own hearts on your beds, and be silent.

Read Proverbs 11:12.
Whoever belittles his neighbor lacks sense, but a man of understanding remains silent.

Read Proverbs 17:28.
Even a fool who keeps silent is considered wise; when he closes his lips, he is deemed intelligent.

From the verses above, when is it best to keep silent?

We need to choose our words wisely and not "cast our 'pearls' before swine." Sometimes it's better to say nothing than to say the wrong thing out of anger or ignorance. But at other times, we must speak up.

Read Ephesians 4:15, 25.
¹⁵Rather, speaking the truth in love, we are to grow up in every way into him who is the head, into Christ,
²⁵Therefore, having put away falsehood, let each one of you speak the truth with his neighbor, for we are members one of another.

✸ How should we speak according to Paul?

Read Proverbs 10:11-13a.
¹¹The mouth of the righteous is a fountain of life, but the mouth of the wicked conceals violence. ¹²Hatred stirs up strife, but love covers all offenses. ¹³On the lips of him who has understanding, wisdom is found…

According to these verses, what guides you when to speak and when to keep silent?

What can get you into trouble?

There is a time to speak for the glory of God and to build up others. The wisdom to know when to speak and when to keep silent comes from spending time in the presence of the heavenly Father who gives us wisdom to know what time it is.

There is also a time for love.

Read Proverbs 17:17.
A friend loves at all times, and a brother is born for adversity.

Read I John 3:11.
For this is the message that you have heard from the beginning, that we should love one another.

Read I John 3:17.
But if anyone has the world's goods and sees his brother in need, yet closes his heart against him, how does God's love abide in him? Little children, let us not love in word or talk but in deed and in truth.

✱ What are practical ways to show love in the verses above?

Read I John 4:7-12.
7Beloved, let us love one another, for love is from God, and whoever loves
has been born of God and knows God. 8Anyone who does not love does not
know God, because God is love. 9In this the love of God was made manifest
among us, that God sent his only Son into the world, so that we might live
through him. 10In this is love, not that we have loved God but that he loved
us and sent his Son to be the propitiation for our sins. 11Beloved, if God
so loved us, we also ought to love one another. 12No one has ever seen God;
if we love one another, God abides in us and his love is perfected in us.

Summarize John's teaching about a time to love.

God is love. When His unconditional, sacrificial love flows through us to others, it brings life. Loving the unlovable is a small taste of experiencing the love of God abiding in our hearts. While the world can't see God, it can experience His love through us.

Then, Solomon tells us, there is a time for hate.

Read Proverbs 8:13.
The fear of the Lord is hatred of evil. Pride and arrogance and the way of evil and perverted speech I hate.

Read Proverbs 13:5.
The righteous hates falsehood, but the wicked brings shame and disgrace.

Read Proverbs 15:27.
Whoever is greedy for unjust gain troubles his own household, but he who hates bribes will live.

Read Proverbs 28:16.
A ruler who lacks understanding is a cruel oppressor, but he who hates unjust gain will prolong his days.

What is it okay to hate?

We must "hate" oppression and injustice and stand up for those who cannot speak up for themselves. Sometimes, it is time for war.

Read Joshua 11:18, 19.
[18]Joshua made war a long time with all those kings. [19]There was not a city that made peace with the people of Israel except the Hivites, the inhabitants of Gibeon. They took them all in battle.

Read Matthew 24:5-7.
[5]For many will come in my name, saying, 'I am the Christ,' and they will lead many astray. [6]And you will hear of wars and rumors of wars. See that you are not alarmed, for this must take place, but the end is not yet. [7]For nation will rise against nation, and kingdom against kingdom, and there will be famines and earthquakes in various places.

When is the time for war?

It is time for war when God calls us to fight for what is right. We pray for peace, but are willing to go to battle against evil. Whenever possible, however, we are to live at peace with our fellow man.

Read Proverbs 12:20.
Deceit is in the heart of those who devise evil, but those who plan peace have joy.

Read Proverbs 16:7.
When a man's ways please the Lord, he makes even his enemies to be at peace with him.

Solomon explains that there is a time to mend relationships that are broken. There is a time to keep silent when words would only pour "gasoline on the fire," and there is a time to speak with Spirit words instructed by the Father. There is a time to love generously and unconditionally, and there is a time to hate what is wrong and stand for righteousness. There is a time when we'll be called upon to go to war to fight for what is right, and there is a time when the swords are sheathed and it is time for peace.

Read Ecclesiastes 3:11-14.
^{11}He has made everything beautiful in its time. Also, he has put eternity into man's heart, yet so that he cannot find out what God has done from the beginning to the end. ^{12}I perceived that there is nothing better for them than to be joyful and to do good as long as they live; ^{13}also that everyone should eat and drink and take pleasure in all his toil—this is God's gift to man. ^{14}I perceived that whatever God does endures forever; nothing can be added to it, nor anything taken from it. God has done it, so that people fear before him.

Fill in the blanks from verse 11:

He had made everything _____ in its time.

Also, he has put _____ into man's heart.

In verses 12 and 13, Solomon lists four things that are the best way to live our lives:

1.

2.

3.

4.

Solomon puts life in perspective as he tells us that "God has made everything beautiful in its time" and that we are to be busy only with the things God has assigned to us. He warns us not to fall into the trap of work becoming our god. Since we were made for eternity, the things of this world cannot fully and permanently satisfy. Verses 12 and 13 are an early pointer to the book's conclusion—that is, God's people are to enjoy life by enjoying food, drink, work, and doing good for others. Life is fleeting, but enjoying simple pleasures are a gift from God.

Solomon has been telling us about life on earth in its simplest terms, and then in verse 14 he takes us up "above the earth" to give us a heavenly perspective. Whatever God does, what He initiates and ordains will endure, and those on earth cannot add or subtract from it. The main point of life on earth is to do what we see our heavenly Father doing, joining Him in His work. Anything we initiate or plan without Him is worthless. That includes ministry plans, church plans, business plans, or family plans. So we must live our lives "under the sun" with simple, childlike faith, enjoying what God gives us to enjoy today—our daily bread, our assignments from Him like caring for our children, going to work to provide for our family, cleaning our homes, teaching Bible studies, or ministering to a neighbor. At the same time, we live "above the sun" with eternity in our hearts, worshipping and adoring our Heavenly Father and His beautiful son.

What time is it?

A Bit of Wisdom

Write a text, email, or send a physical card to someone who needs your love right now. Maybe you can even order flowers or cookies to be delivered to their doorstep. Stop and ask God who He wants you to love in His name. You can be a channel of unconditional love and blessing, and you never know how God will use a simple message to reach the heart of someone who is hurting.

BIBLE STUDY NOTES

WEEK 5
HOW SHOULD I MANAGE MY RESOURCES AND PREPARE MY HEIRS?

A Personal Message to You from Solomon

Wisdom, words, women, and wealth are subjects I studied in depth; and I have a few things to share with you on those subjects that can save you a lot of trouble. Trust me. I've experienced the wrong and the right way to enjoy these things. Your words, your relationships and your wealth will outlive you, so what you do now to invest in them wisely will make an impact on generations to come. Be smart and follow the path I will show to you.

Overcoming Oppression

Day 1

Lord, today I worship You, love You, and bow down to You. Open my eyes and my heart to see the people of this world who are under oppression. Give me instruction for how to pray and how to help. Lord, You see every tear that falls. Show me the way to bring comfort, hope, and peace to those who are suffering. Forgive my self-centeredness and give me a heart that is merciful and ready to serve. Thank You for all that You have done for me, Lord. You are my all in all, Lord Jesus. It is in Your name I pray. Amen.

Madeline watched the news with a broken heart for the people of her adopted land. The oppressive government brought pain and suffering for the people she loved. How could she help them? This morning, she spent more time than usual on her knees, asking God for specific instruction on how to alleviate some of the hardships for her neighbors. She couldn't change the laws, but she could bring hope and healing to the hurting. In her quiet way, she would bring a "Jesus revolution" in her neighborhood, one household at a time. While she had to be very careful about openly sharing the gospel, she could love unconditionally in Jesus' name. No one could stop that. And love has a way of overcoming barriers and tearing down walls that some would think impossible. When she arose from her prayer time, she had renewed vision and energy for what lay ahead.

Read Ecclesiastes 4:1-3.

¹Again, I saw all the oppressions that are done under the sun. And behold, the tears of the oppressed, and they had no one to comfort them! On the side of their oppressors there was power, and there was no one to comfort them. ²And I thought the dead who are already dead more fortunate than the living who are still alive. ³But better than both is he who has not yet been and has not seen the evil deeds that are done under the sun.

Google to find the word "oppression" and give the definition here.

What oppressive circumstances do you see in our world today as you watch the news?

When have you felt under mental oppression from your own circumstances?

The Bible doesn't wince at being honest about life when it's hard. Solomon observed life under the sun and told us that sometimes those who are powerful oppress those who are subject to their authority. Oppression happens when there are unjust, cruel actions taken on helpless victims. Oppression can happen on a national scale with a totalitarian government, on a local scale with an unfair boss who is a tyrant with his subordinates, or when an abusive parent torments his or her own family.

Week 5: Day 1

One way I experienced oppression was from a teacher I had in school who chose to repeatedly humiliate me in front of the class. It's been 50 years, but I still remember in vivid detail the way her cruelty completely changed the way I saw myself and how I felt about school for years—and not in a good way. When Solomon observes the "tears of the oppressed" and how they couldn't find comfort, it resonates with me when I remember my hurt. Jesus never promised a stress-free life but warned us that life on earth would be full of trouble. However, with Jesus, there is always comfort, peace and hope.

Read John 16:33.
I have said these things to you, that in me you may have peace. In the world you will have tribulation. But take heart; I have overcome the world.

Which two words in the verse above guarantee our hope?

We find our hope *in* Jesus. When we are oppressed and downtrodden, we find our peace in our relationship with Him. He will never change and He is always there. That's why our peace doesn't depend on our circumstances.

Re-read what Paul writes in Romans 8:35-39.
³⁵Who shall separate us from the love of Christ? Shall tribulation, or distress, or persecution, or famine, or nakedness, or danger, or sword? ³⁶As it is written, "For your sake we are being killed all the day long; we are regarded as sheep to be slaughtered." ³⁷No, in all these things we are more than conquerors through him who loved us. ³⁸For I am sure that neither death nor life, nor angels nor rulers, nor things present nor things to come, nor powers, ³⁹nor height nor depth, nor anything else in all creation, will be able to separate us from the love of God in Christ Jesus our Lord.

Which circumstances can separate you from the love of Jesus?

Fill in the blanks of verse 37:

No, in all these things we are _____

_____

_____through him who loved us.

Read Luke 4:18, 19 to discover that Jesus' first sermon declared that He came to release those who are oppressed.

¹⁸The Spirit of the Lord is upon me, because he has anointed me to proclaim good news to the poor. He has sent me to proclaim liberty to the captives and recovery of sight to the blind, to set at liberty those who are oppressed, ¹⁹to proclaim the year of the Lord's favor.

Jesus outlined his ministry objectives in these verses. List each one:

1.

2.

3.

4.

5.

Jesus came to set us free! He had just spent 40 days and nights in the wilderness, being tempted by Satan under oppressive and repeated onslaughts of spiritual attacks. He emerged from that experience to begin His earthly ministry and declared His mission: to bring good news to the poor, to set at liberty the oppressed and captives, to bring about recovery for the blind, and to proclaim the Lord's favor.

Oppression of Toil

Read Ecclesiastes 4:4-6.
⁴Then I saw that all toil and all skill in work come from a man's envy of his neighbor. This also is vanity and a striving after wind. ⁵The fool folds his hands and eats his own flesh. ⁶Better is a handful of quietness than two hands full of toil and a striving after wind.

What kind of worker do we find in verse 4?

What kind of worker do we find in verse 5?

What is Solomon's conclusion about work in verse 6?

Both overwork and underwork are their own kind of oppression. Neither over-work (motivated by envy) nor idleness brings happiness, meaning, or fulfillment. The answer is to find a healthy balance, content with "one handful" of life's provisions rather than grasping for both hands to be full at any cost.

Read Colossians 3:23, 24.
²³Whatever you do, work heartily, as for the Lord and not for men, ²⁴knowing that from the Lord you will receive the inheritance as your reward. You are serving the Lord Christ.

What is our motivation to work?

Who is our ultimate "boss?"

In a season in the wilderness, we especially need to be balanced in our work and remain quiet in our hearts before the Lord, content in whatever circumstance we find ourselves.

In Philippians 4:11-13, Paul describes a life of "quietness and contentment."
¹¹Not that I am speaking of being in need, for I have learned in whatever situation I am to be content. ¹²I know how to be brought low, and I know how to abound. In any and every circumstance, I have learned the secret of facing plenty and hunger, abundance and need. ¹³I can do all things through him who strengthens me.

Fill in the blank from verse 11:

I have learned in whatever _____ I am to be _____.

Solomon's lesson for us is to keep our work in perspective by staying in balance. Peace and contentment is found when we don't work too much or too little.

Oppression of Loneliness

Read Ecclesiastes 4:7-12.
⁷Again, I saw vanity under the sun: ⁸one person who has no other, either son or brother, yet there is no end to all his toil, and his eyes are never satisfied with riches, so that he never asks, "For whom am I toiling and depriving myself of pleasure?" This also is vanity and an unhappy business. ⁹Two are better than one, because they have a good reward for their toil. ¹⁰For if they fall, one will lift up his fellow. But woe to him who is alone when he falls and has not another to lift him up! ¹¹Again, if two lie together, they keep warm, but how can one keep warm alone? ¹²And though a man might prevail against one who is alone, two will withstand him—a threefold cord is not quickly broken.

❋ What is the new "vanity under the sun" that Solomon identifies in these verses?

✶ What is Solomon's solution to being alone?

✶ List several phrases from verses 9-12 that resonate with you and write down the circumstance in your life or that of a loved one who needs the truth in these verses. Stop and pray for God to bring unity and love into that situation.

_____

_____

_____

Living life independently might sound easier and less complicated, but a lonely life is ultimately not a happy one. While many will marry and have a life-long companion, more and more people in our world today live the single life. Some of you started a Winter Season when you suddenly became single. Some by choice, but for many it is the last thing you want.

What if marriage is not an option for you right now? Perhaps you've never found "the right one" or you found your love, but they are gone due to death or divorce. Whether being single is by your choice or not, Solomon gives us wisdom on how to manage our loneliness. He tells us to find someone to share our life. There are children and the elderly who need loving support. There are single moms, grandmothers, and widows who also need companions.

And if your heart desires a mate, then ask God to bring the right person at the right time, trusting and waiting for Him to provide. Stay sexually pure until that day arrives. "Moving in" with someone before marriage isn't the answer you're looking for. It will bring temporary relief from loneliness, but the guilt of "living in sin" will eat at your conscience and rob you of joy. God will provide what your heart needs if you will let Him. Trust and obey Him to satisfy your needs, and He will abundantly supply.

Solomon tells us that two are better than one. He explains that if you fall, you'll have someone to help you up; and if you are cold, you'll have someone to keep you warm. For those of you who are married, you already know that marital unity takes a lot of work.

Some of you had Ecclesiastes 4:9-12 read at your wedding, but you had no idea what that would require of you. To have oneness in your marriage where you lift each other up, you'll need to sacrifice your singleness, selfishness, and self-centeredness on the altar. To "keep each other warm" you'll need to share everything you have because it's no longer "mine" but "ours." Experiencing the "threefold cord that is not quickly broken" happens when husband and wife join the Lord Jesus in a holy union of hearts bound by His love. Couples experience this unity of Spirit the most when they pray together before the throne of God.

In 1965, Burt Bacharach and Hal David wrote the song "What the world needs now, is love, sweet love," and it's truer now than when they wrote it. Everyone needs someone to love, and everyone needs love. There are hearts waiting for your love, and you will be richer and happier if you will give it away.

A Bit of Wisdom

The best way to make friends is to be a good friend. Can I encourage you to find at least one woman to be your prayer partner? The Covid-19 pandemic taught us something important about using Zoom to gather people for prayer. I set up a Zoom meeting with our prayer partners, and we prayed together for healing—not only for me but for all those suffering. We expanded our prayer times to include personal requests from each of us and Kardo ministry prayer concerns. We used Scripture as the basis for our prayers and met together every day for a while, then later every week at the same time. We set up a group text so that we could send updates. Our prayer team has never been stronger and more bonded. Prayer is our most powerful ally as we go through life together.

Not only were we able to pray on Zoom, David and I also spoke for Zoom conferences in Bolivia and Mongolia, teaching and training leaders, families, and women's groups to hundreds of people through technology. God is opening doors to serve more families than ever before.

WORDS — Day 2

Lord Jesus, I pray that my words would be instructed by Your Spirit. Forgive me, Lord, when I speak rashly and use my words to hurt others. I ask You to fill my heart with love, joy, peace, and patience and to let that flow through my words. Lord, prompt me when I need to restrain my tongue. I ask all this in the name of Jesus. Amen.

ABIGAIL AND JOHN were actively involved in the lives of their six adult children and their precious new grandbaby, managed their busy restaurant with all the employees and sat on several committees at church. They were both high-energy, get-it-done kind of people who fed off challenges. When they built an additional restaurant in a new location across town, they prayed over every brick and piece of wood and wrote Scripture in the foundation. One night, as they prayed before they went to bed, they begged God to bless their expanding business. John decided to put some weight behind his prayer, so he committed to the Lord the entire first month's profit from their establishment. Knowing all the bills they had incurred, they both gulped when they realized what he had just prayed. John sort of hoped God hadn't been listening to his prayers that night. But both John and Abigail knew it was important to keep their promise to God.

Read Ecclesiastes 5:1-7.

✷ What instruction does Solomon give us about our mouths?

1.

2.

3.

4.

Solomon uses graphic word pictures to warn us to guard our steps and guard our tongues. He speaks to us about speaking too much and too rashly—especially in our vows before Almighty God. We are to humbly enter into God's presence with reverence and respect of who God is and who we are.

Solomon also gives instruction about our words from his book of Proverbs.

Read Proverbs 10:19.
When words are many, transgression is not lacking, but whoever restrains his lips is prudent.

Read Proverbs 12:18.
There is one whose rash words are like sword thrusts, but the tongue of the wise brings healing.

Read Proverbs 17:27.
Whoever restrains his words has knowledge, and he who has a cool spirit is a man of understanding.

What are the lessons about our words in these verses?

Read Proverbs 15:1-7.

¹A soft answer turns away wrath, but a harsh word stirs up anger. ²The tongue of the wise commends knowledge, but the mouths of fools pour out folly. ³The eyes of the LORD are in every place, keeping watch on the evil and the good. ⁴A gentle tongue is a tree of life, but perverseness in it breaks the spirit. ⁵A fool despises his father's instruction, but whoever heeds reproof is prudent. ⁶In the house of the righteous there is much treasure, but trouble befalls the income of the wicked. ⁷The lips of the wise spread knowledge; not so the hearts of fools.

✸ List every word that pertains to "words and speaking" and write beside it the instruction of Scripture.

1. Example: Soft answer- turns away wrath

2. Example: Harsh word- stirs up anger

3.

4.

5.

6.

7.

8.

9.

Read Proverbs 16:24.

Gracious words are like a honeycomb, sweetness to the soul and health to the body.

Proverbs 18:4.

The words of a man's mouth are deep waters; the fountain of wisdom is a bubbling brook.

> What are the word pictures in these verses referring to your words? Make a simple drawing to help you understand the concepts.

Our words can be sharp or soft, damaging or healing, bridge-builders or deadly demolishers. Think before you speak. Edit your comments before they are spoken. Pray diligently over your words that they would bring life not death to your hearers, especially to those in your own household.

A Bit of Wisdom

Start a small spiral notebook and copy in Scriptures about your words. Keep this little book near your Bible for your morning devotionals. Try to memorize one Scripture each week about your mouth and your words. Then at the back of your notebook, write down the good experiences you have after applying the lessons you've learned.

True Inheritance — Day 3

Lord, thank You for Your bountiful blessings and provision. Forgive me for focusing on the gifts you give to me, rather than on my love relationship with You, my Creator. Speak truth to me through Your Word. It is in Your name I pray, Amen.

ELIZABETH was the money manager of the family, not only of her own finances since Stephen's death, but she also handled all of her parents' money. Of all the sisters, she was best at paying their bills, and she banked remotely for them until both of them passed away. She was more aware than most of the importance of planning how to transfer wealth from one generation to another. She saw both the good planning and the mistakes her parents made in how to fairly and generously leave money and possessions to the next generation. She was determined to do better for her own children. She knew an inheritance can bless or curse those who receive it. It can lead to fighting between siblings or bring them closer together. Elizabeth understood that wise money management and planning is not just for this life but also for after you are gone.

Read Ecclesiastes 5:10-12.

¹⁰He who loves money will not be satisfied with money, nor he who loves wealth with his income; this also is vanity. ¹¹When goods increase, they increase who eat them, and what advantage has their owner but to see them with his eyes? ¹²Sweet is the sleep of a laborer, whether he eats little or much, but the full stomach of the rich will not let him sleep.

Which "vanity" or meaningless activity does Solomon explain in this passage?

How is the laborer contrasted with the rich man?

Read Ecclesiastes 5:13-16.

What did Solomon find to be a "grievous evil" in verses 13 and 14?

✹ Mark the following True or False:

_____ If I could have more money, I'd be satisfied.

_____ Shopping is my favorite pastime, and I can't seem to stop.

_____ I'm happy with our income.

_____ I'm constantly worrying about money.

_____ I'm a good saver, but I need to save a lot more.

What from the list above would you like to change?

Solomon reminds us all of how we came into this world and how we will leave…with NOTHING! The story is told of the question asked of John D. Rockefeller's accountant after he died, "I wonder how much he left for his heirs?" And the answer was, "He left it ALL!"

When it comes to fully experiencing wealth and riches, Solomon of all men has the right to say, "Been there, done that!" He had it all, and he tells us that money is a blessing, but it can also get us into trouble. Many of us work for it, spend it, save it, think about it, and worry about having enough.

Our 21st century society will tell us if we have more money, we'll be happier because the solution to most of our problems is to have wealth. But Solomon makes it clear that greater wealth does not bring satisfaction and in fact, he says in verse 10 that greater wealth can bring greater anxiety and worry. He was the wealthiest man who ever lived and had everything his heart desired.

He looks back through history to tell us that money won't satisfy the ache in your soul. It cannot provide what you really need.

Solomon reminds us that we had absolutely nothing when we entered this world, and we will leave everything behind when we die. God provides everything for us from the moment of birth and carries us through this life with His provision. It all belongs to Him, and there is no reason for covetousness, since both the rich man and the poor man end up just the same.

Paul understood this well and instructed his disciple Timothy with these words in I Timothy 6:6-10:

⁶But godliness with contentment is great gain, ⁷for we brought nothing into the world, and we cannot take anything out of the world. ⁸But if we have food and clothing, with these we will be content. ⁹But those who desire to be rich fall into temptation, into a snare, into many senseless and harmful desires that plunge people into ruin and destruction. ¹⁰For the love of money is a root of all kinds of evils. It is through this craving that some have wandered away from the faith and pierced themselves with many pangs.

What is the formula for greatest gain given in verse 6?

✦ Which concepts are common between Ecclesiastes 5:13-16 and I Timothy 6:6-10?

✦ What are the two things we really need in order to be content in life according to verse 8?

Week 5: Day 3

✺ Give an example of someone you know of who embodies I Timothy 6:6-8.

Write the initials of someone you know who embodies I Timothy 6:9-10.

What can you learn from their lives?

Fill in the blanks from verse 10: "For the _____ of _____ is a root of all kinds of evil…"

Unfortunately, even some believers have "pierced themselves with many pangs" through "craving" money. But that is not the way of joy and peace. If the love of money is a stronghold in your life that needs to come down, spend some time with the Lord dealing with it in prayer. Solomon urges us to live life in freedom and joy, enjoying the simple things of life.

Read Ecclesiastes 5:18-20.

✺ What is a "good and fitting" way to live your life?

✹ What is the gift from God named in these verses?

There are some things that are certain for every person:
1. We will all die.
2. We don't know how much time we have left, and the day of death will probably not be our choice.
3. We won't take anything with us.
4. Our money and possessions will pass to our heirs.
5. We can only decide who gets our things before we die, not after.

Wisely managing your financial resources while you're alive and then wisely transferring wealth to the next generation takes incredible discernment, it takes facing your own death, it requires you to let go of fear and control, and causes you to lean into God's leading like never before in your life. Solomon reminds us that "we can't take it with us" and preparing for the day our children and/or ministries and charities will inherit what we have saved is a necessary part of the Winter Season.

There is a balance between providing for your family with an inheritance and furthering God's kingdom purposes even after your death. Many of us learned lessons from the poverty of early marriage where we were living on love and not much else. Let's not take away those lessons from our children by giving them "too much." We need to avoid solving our adult children's problems by "buying" solutions. The inheritance our children receive should be a great blessing to them.

You can decide what impact you will have on your family and God's kingdom both while you live and after you die. Imagine what could happen on the mission field with a gift from your estate. Begin praying now for God to inspire you with His plan.

A Bit of Wisdom

Here are some of the opportunities and challenges of wealth transfer:

- Providing for your spouse
- Providing for God's kingdom purposes
- Deciding which ministries and charities to support
- Helping your children and grandchildren without harming them
- Managing expectations of spouse and children
- Dealing with in-laws (daughters-in-law, sons-in-law, brothers and sisters-in-law, stepchildren, step-grandchildren, etc.)
- Avoiding family conflict and sibling rivalry
- Dealing with the reality of your death
- Coming to terms with the fact that all your hard-earned wealth and all your prized possessions will go to someone else
- Handling changes in family dynamics and adjusting your estate plans accordingly
- Learning about complex legal and financial matters, such as wills, trusts, and estate taxes, etc.
- Desiring to finish strong

[Adapted from *Splitting Heirs (Giving Your Money and Things to Your Children Without Ruining Their Lives)* by Ron Blue with Jeremy White]

SCROOGE VS. CRATCHIT
Day 4

Lord, I bless Your name today, giving You glory, honor, and praise. I bow before You, Heavenly Father. Thank You for Your blessings and provision. Forgive me for sinful attitudes and motives in handling money. Please show me the way to lay up treasures in heaven rather than treasures on earth. You are my Shepherd, and I am committing my financial resources into Your hands. I pray all this in Jesus' name, Amen.

THE SISTERS had grown up loving Dickens' *A Christmas Carol*. It was a Christmas tradition to read it together as family and then watch one of the many movies made from this story. Ebenezer Scrooge, the iconic stingy figure in the 1843 novel is a picture of Ecclesiastes 5:13-17. The contrast between Scrooge and Bob Cratchit is a picture of folly versus wisdom about wealth. Bitter, and finding no pleasure in life while hoarding his money, Ebenezer finally turned from his folly to generous giving and found true joy.

Read Ecclesiastes 6:1-6a.

The rich man is compared to a _____ if he doesn't enjoy his own blessings that God has given to him.

What is the common key word in verses 2 and 6?

What is the "evil" Solomon sees under the sun in these verses?

In verse 3, even though a man has everything, including 100 children (which Solomon probably had at least that many!), if he is "not _____ with good things," he's no better off than someone who is dead.

You may not consider yourself "wealthy" when you compare yourself to Jeff Bezos (the founder of Amazon), Bill Gates (Co-founder of Microsoft), or Warren Buffet (the "Oracle of Omaha"), known for his prowess in investing. These men have amassed unimaginable fortunes of billions of dollars. That probably won't be you. But compared to most of the people on earth who live in survival mode for basic food and shelter, you are probably very wealthy. If you live in a house that you own or an apartment where you always pay the rent, you are wealthy. If you have plenty to eat and plenty of clothes to wear, you are wealthy. If you can take vacations and pay for your child's education, you are very wealthy. But what if you have all of these things and still aren't satisfied with the amount of money in your accounts and never stop stockpiling long enough to enjoy your blessings?

Solomon warns us from his experience. He was the top billionaire of his day and had absolutely everything money could buy, but his heart was never satisfied with all these things. Can you even imagine his lavish lifestyle? Not only did Solomon have almost all of the wealth of his world, he had the absolute power and authority to keep it for himself. However, after all of this, he laments that it doesn't satisfy.

Do you know why this kind of wealth doesn't satisfy our souls? Why it leaves us empty and aching for something more when we can buy anything we want? It's because wealth was never meant to be an end in itself. It is a means for doing good in the world, for being God's messenger of hope and help, and of encouragement and embrace. Money is meant to DO something, not to just pile up in financial accounts to make us feel proud and secure. That will never fill our hearts.

One of the key principles of money and possessions is found in the verses below:

Read Job 41:11b
Whatever is under the whole heaven is mine.

Read I Chronicles 29:14, where King David says:
14But who am I, and what is my people, that we should be able thus to offer willingly? For all things come from you, and of your own have we given you.

Read Deuteronomy 8:18a.
18You shall remember the Lord Your God, for it is he who gives you power to get wealth.

❈ What did you learn about your money from these verses?

God owns it all; we are just His stewards and money managers. In his book, *The Treasure Principle*, Randy Alcorn says we are God's errand boys and delivery girls. We just work here; we don't own the place. Suppose you have something important you want to get to someone who needs it. You wrap it up and hand it over to the FedEx person. What would you think if instead of delivering the package, he or she took it home, opened it, and kept it? You'd say, "The package doesn't belong to you. You're just the middleman. Your job is to get it from me to the person I want you to deliver it to." Just because God put His money in our hands doesn't mean He intends for it to stay there![1]

Truly believing that God owns it all has three implications:
1. He can take whatever He wants whenever He wants.
2. Every spending decision is a spiritual decision.
3. Stewardship cannot be faked.

Read Luke 6:38.

Give, and it will be given to you. Good measure, pressed down, shaken together, running over, will be put into your lap. For with the measure you use it will be measured back to you.

What additional principle for managing your money do you find in this verse?

How much will return to you when you give?

Read Luke 18:18-25.

18And a ruler asked him, "Good Teacher, what must I do to inherit eternal life?" 19And Jesus said to him, "Why do you call me good? No one is good except God alone. 20You know the commandments: 'Do not commit adultery, Do not murder, Do not steal, Do not bear false witness, Honor your father and mother.'" 21And he said, "All these I have kept from my youth." 22When Jesus heard this, he said to him, "One thing you still lack. Sell all that you have and distribute to the poor, and you will have treasure in heaven; and come, follow me." 23But when he heard these things, he became very sad, for he was extremely rich. 24Jesus, seeing that he had become sad, said, "How difficult it is for those who have wealth to enter the kingdom of God! 25For it is easier for a camel to go through the eye of a needle than for a rich person to enter the kingdom of God."

What challenge did Jesus lay before the ruler?

Why didn't the man take the challenge?

The young ruler's love of money was a stumbling block to following Jesus. Jesus knew the man needed to rid himself of his idols and urged him to sell everything to become a disciple. That man has gone down in history—in fact, you and I still talk about his choice—knowing he held on to what he could not take with him and turned away from an invitation to walk the earth with the very Son of God. Just think about what he turned down: talking with Jesus in human form every day, asking Him questions, hearing God's truth and living in His presence.

Few men who have ever lived had that privilege. And he turned it down because he wouldn't give away his money. Giving away our money will bring us joy because it sets our hearts free. The more we give, the more God will entrust to us and the more we are able to give again.

God designed us to be His emissaries and to use the resources entrusted to us to bring light into the dark world. No matter what you own—whether it's a little or a lot—you can have the joy of giving. And if your Winter Season means you are in the final quarter of life, you'll need to get busy distributing the resources God has given to you. You will experience the fullness and joy of life when you start opening your heart and giving away your treasures to your family, your church, ministries and charities, and individuals who need your encouragement and help.

Your gift may be large or small. It might be having dinner delivered to a sick friend from their favorite restaurant. Your gift might be a small donation to a grandchild's university savings fund as an investment in their future. If you have the ability, you might give your church needed equipment for online streaming services or new instruments for the worship team. You might know a ministry that keeps a running Amazon Wish List. Visit it each quarter and buy even one or two small items that will be a practical help and a great encouragement. If you see a young mom in line before you at the grocery store who is struggling to pay for her groceries, pay her bill. Give and give generously, and you will discover the JOY of enjoying your wealth.

Solomon speaks of the disappointment we might experience if a stranger enjoyed the wealth God entrusted to us. Let me ask you a question: How well do you know your own heirs? Are any of them strangers to you? It is the time now to get to know your heirs and to begin training them to be generous with their time, talent and treasure. Think about encouraging their spiritual growth by paying for Christian camp or retreats. Maybe you can help out with Christian school tuition. Or better yet, take them on a mission trip and serve alongside them.

Remember, you can choose the impact your wealth will have on the world. Your goal is to invest in lives, hearts, and families for generations to come. Prayerfully discuss your giving strategy with your spouse, if you are married. (Don't give their money without their permission!) If you're single, talk to a trusted friend and prayer partner and seek professional advice. Solomon tells us how many times a stranger enjoys the wealth, possessions and honor of some who die without a plan for giving. Don't let that be you. Pour into those whom God brings onto your path now so you can bless them and, in turn, be abundantly blessed!

[1] *The Treasure Principle*, Randy Alcorn, Multnomah Publishers, 2001, p 74.

A Bit of Wisdom

We wrote about giving priorities in our Kardo Bible study, *Keeping the Secrets of Jesus*:

1. Give first to the Lord: Tithe 10 percent of your gross income (before taxes) to your local church body as the first expenditure each month.

2. Give next to your family: Care generously for the needs of your own family, without spoiling them.

3. Give to the body of Christ worldwide: Ask God to make you aware of the needs of His children around the world and places where you can "lay up treasures in heaven."

4. Give to the poor and needy: Find a ministry that you trust that ministers to the poor. Look for opportunities to help in a way that is a "hand up" to supporting themselves, not a "hand out."

5. Give to your "enemies." "You have heard that it was said, 'Love your neighbor and hate your enemy.' But I tell you: Love your enemies and pray for those who persecute you that you may be sons of your Father in heaven..." Matthew 5:43-48.

Take a practical step of faith by giving to one or many of those listed here. You'll find your heart filling with JOY!

(You'll find *Keeping the Secrets of Jesus* on our website at kardo.org.)

BIBLE STUDY NOTES

Preparing Your Heirs
Day 5

Lord Jesus, You have all authority in heaven and on earth. I bow and submit to Your Lordship over my heart, my possessions, my relationships, and my whole life. Teach me how to prepare those who will come after me. Show me how to train them to follow You in all Your ways. Lord, use me and all those who will follow me when I'm gone, to accomplish everything in Your heart and mind for us to do. Lord, I pray to finish strong and to leave a legacy of love and faith. Show me the way. I love You so much, Lord Jesus. Amen.

ELIZABETH had finally finished all the paperwork following Stephen's death. It was painful, emotional, and hard work. But the legacy of this wonderful man made the tedious tasks more bearable. He had prepared well for his homegoing. All the bills were paid, money had been set aside for Elizabeth's care, and he had kept immaculate records of every account, all the insurance policies, and the deeds to the house and cars. He had even made a secret notebook known only to her of all his login usernames and passwords. That little book was a key to making life easier for Elizabeth and her children to navigate the unknown waters of the death of their loved one.

Stephen had prepared them in a way most men don't have the courage to do. He had called a family meeting a couple of years before his death and openly talked with Elizabeth and the children about his finances and his desires and plans for the time when he would leave them. At the time, they joked and teased and tried to laugh away the inevitable truth that someday their dad would be gone. They imagined that it would be many, many years, and maybe even decades, in the future. They could not have known that the day would arrive in less than two years.

At the family meeting, Stephen shared with them his testimony of how God had provided over and over again for Elizabeth and him through good times and bad. He told them his personal mission statement and philosophy of managing money and of giving. He told them how he hoped and prayed that they would follow God's call and be world-changers. He asked them to use the money they would receive as an inheritance to benefit their families and to advance God's kingdom. They ended the meeting in prayer and joyful tears. He passed on wisdom to his heirs before he passed on his wealth.

Read Proverbs 13:22.

A good man leaves an inheritance to his children's children, but the sinner's wealth is laid up for the righteous.

Early in his life, Solomon notes how wealth is to be passed from one generation to another. He counsels grandparents to pass blessings to their heirs. But later in life, he realizes his own heirs are unprepared to receive and faithfully use the resources that will be passed to them at his death. You can almost hear him groan as he writes about what will happen after he is gone.

Read Ecclesiastes 6:7, 8 and 12.

[7]All the toil of man is for his mouth, yet his appetite is not satisfied. [8]For what advantage has the wise man over the fool?

[12]For who knows what is good for man while he lives the few days of his vain life, which he passes like a shadow? For who can tell man what will be after him under the sun?

✷ What things does Solomon list in this passage as a source of despair?

✷ What is Solomon questioning in verse 12?

These are the things we learned from Ecclesiastes 6:7-12.

1. The short-lived rewards of life (v 7)
2. The debatable rewards of life (v 8)
3. The elusive rewards of life (v 9)
4. The limits of our creativity, power, and wisdom (v 10-11)[1]

Solomon almost despairs of life as he considers how to spend his days and how to prepare his heirs for the future. While most of us stay so busy we don't take time to consider what will happen to our family when we are gone, the time is now to take stock of what we are doing with our lives, what we can do to make an impact on God's kingdom, and how to prepare our heirs. We need to bravely and prayerfully make plans with a will and the legal documents they will someday need. We need to decide who will settle our affairs as the executor of our will. Will it be a family member or an attorney or someone at a bank? This person will ensure your heirs receive their inheritance. If you have children still living at home, you will need to appoint a trusted guardian to care for them.

You need to answer the questions: Who? What? When? Where? Why? And how? about what will happen after you are gone. Let's take them one at a time.

♦ Who?

We need to decide who will receive our earthly goods after we pass from this life. Discuss with your mate or a trusted advisor who will be your heirs. Authors Ron Blue and Randy Alcorn remind us that for most people, they automatically assume their children will inherit everything, but they encourage us to think carefully and prayerfully about leaving an inheritance only to our children and grandchildren. In some families, a large inheritance could possibly harm them if they lose the motivation to work or use the money to finance a lifestyle that is detrimental to them. Sometimes the dividing of an estate causes sibling rivalry and destroys the family unity. Christian financial counselors ask us to consider the ministries and charities we want to support in our will. They tell us that if a person has considerable wealth (a house, some financial accounts, etc.) and/or precious heirlooms, they need to think about each child's life individually and answer these questions:

1. What would be the best and worst outcome of their receiving an inheritance from you?

2. Will they use your hard-earned, carefully managed resources for the benefit of themselves and their families and to invest further in God's kingdom, or will they squander the money and hurt themselves? [2]

Ron Blue encourages us to "love our children equally, but treat them individually. If one child is a single mother trying to provide for her children, you might help her more than your child who is a doctor. If one of your children has serious health issues requiring expensive medical treatments, it might be wise to set aside money for those needs."[3]

After you have prayerfully considered each child and how to express unconditional love to them individually, discuss your decision with your family. When you answer the question of who will receive your possessions, be sure to include advancing God's kingdom in your plans for leaving your money. Update your will accordingly at regular intervals.

♦ What?

You may not realize all the many possessions you have in your name. Take time to think it through, create an inventory list, and ask God to show you how to transfer those things in a way that glorifies Him. You might want to start giving some things now or wait until the family reads your will. But prayerfully offer each item to the Lord and listen for His voice on how and to whom to entrust it. Consider your answers to these questions:

1. If you were to die next week, what do you want to happen to your house? How could it do the most good?

2. What passed to you from previous generations? Who in your family is most likely to care for the heirloom and pass it, and the stories that go with it, to the next generations?

3. What do you have that could be better used by someone else right now? Is there anything in your house you are likely to never use again? Can you give it away?

4. What items in your house will your children throw away? Why don't you do that job for them now?

♦ When?

You don't have to wait until you die to give an inheritance to your children and grandchildren. In the United States, we can give monetary gifts to our children at a certain amount each year that are exempt from the gift tax. Perhaps you realize they actually need it more now than they will at your death, which might be when they are already in their 60's. They may be paying for their children's education or a wedding and a gift to them now would mean much more than when they have an empty nest and are already retired themselves. Or they may need help to buy a house, and you have the ability to help out a little bit. Consider these questions:

1. What can you give now to your family that would be timelier than in the future?

2. What can you give to a ministry that needs your help now?

Perhaps you need the money now or you are saving for your care when you are elderly. There is no set formula or one right way to answer the question of, "When?" Ask your heavenly Father and seek His will, and He will let you know through reading His Word, by praying, and listening to wise counsel.

♦ Where?

Where should your money go? That can actually spark some exciting conversations with your mate as you decide where your earthly possessions can do the "utmost for God's highest!" You know you won't take it with you after you die, but you can direct the path of where God's blessings can be channeled for His glory. Think about and discuss these questions:

1. Would it hurt your children if you give all or part of their inheritance to a charity, or would they agree with that plan?

2. Do some of your children need more help than others? How will you communicate your plans with the other children?

3. What do you want to build into the lives of your children and grandchildren, and how can you direct your funds to those objectives?

4. If your extended family has everything they need and you decide as a family to fund a God-sized project, write it in your will. If you have many grandchildren and can help each of them go on mission trips, that's a great way to direct God's resources. You can have fun dreaming and planning and listening to God's heart about where your treasures can be invested for the greatest kingdom good.

♦ **Why?**

Write out your personal mission statement to answer the "why" question about the inheritance that will go to your heirs. It should be a simple sentence that expresses your mission in life. Use these questions to help you formulate your statement:

1. What is your passion? What excites you and fires you up?

2. With what has God burdened your heart?

3. What do you want most to accomplish in this life before you leave it?

Take some time to thoughtfully write out your mission statement and put a copy of it in your lock box at the bank or in your safe. Communicate it to your family so they know your heart's desires before you pass on.

♦ How?

David and I are not financial experts, but we are wise enough to have a godly, Christian financial advisor who gives us expert advice about our money and planning for our heirs. We have read and tried to apply to our lives many books by Ron Blue, Larry Burkett, Dave Ramsey, Randy Alcorn, and many other Christian experts in money management. The time is now to educate yourself on how to leverage your wealth and transfer it in a way that glorifies God. Even if you have very little, you can maximize what you have so you'll leave a legacy when God calls you home.

The process of making these decisions may take many months, but the more you plan and communicate with your family, the better chance you have of a smooth transition of wealth from one generation to the next. Then, there's a greater possibility that you, unlike Solomon, will be able to smile at the future and bless those who will come after you.

[1] *Commentary on the Whole Bible* by Matthew Henry, Edited by Rev. Leslie F. Church, Phd., F.R. Hist.S., Zondervan Publishing House, Grand Rapids, Michigan, 1961, p. 800.

[2] *The Treasure Principle*, Randy Alcorn, Multnomah Publishers.

[3] *Splitting Heirs: Giving Your Money and Your Things to Your Children Without Ruining Their Lives*, Ron Blue, Northfield Publishing.

A Bit of Wisdom

> Evaluate your savings for the future. Have you saved at least six months of income in case you cannot work? Have you saved enough for your care when you are older? How will you save adequately without hoarding?

WEEK 6
WHEN LIFE IS SHORT
HOW CAN I MAKE THE MOST OF IT?

A Personal Message to You from Solomon

You might be surprised to discover that I am well acquainted with suffering. While on the outside it looks like I have had everything imaginable, every life has its share of pain. On top of physical suffering, there is also emotional suffering when life just isn't fair. I looked at suffering from every angle; and while it's not what any of us would choose, there is an upside to this dark side of life. If you will look with me, you'll see what I mean.

Pain & Suffering — Day 1

Lord, hear my cry as I come to You with my pain and hurt. Since You are acquainted with grief, You understand my suffering and comfort me. Jesus, You are sovereign and completely in control, and I put my trust in You. Give me the grace I need to learn through these difficult times. In Jesus' name I pray. Amen.

Abigail, the eldest sister, loved life and everyone around her. While her sisters called her "Mom, Jr." because she mothered them all, she shrugged it off with a laugh. She did love being a mother, even though her own precious children were now into young adulthood, making lives of their own. One day, as Abigail was helping her daughter organize the pantry in her new apartment, the young woman cried out and fainted in her arms. Calling for emergency assistance, Abigail began to fervently pray. She alerted her sisters to begin interceding as she sped away to the hospital, holding her daughter's hand in the back of the ambulance. That day marked the beginning of a long road of suffering for her daughter and for Abigail. Confusing diagnoses, experimental treatments, and months of living in a fog of pain characterized their days. If only she could take the illness away and set her daughter free! Abigail called out the prayer warriors she knew. She fasted and cried out to God for healing and release from pain and misery for her child. But up to now, no relief came. In fact, things got worse. What was God doing? What was He trying to say?

Abigail turned to the Word of God to make some sense of the situation. She'd been clinging to the hope of healing for so long that now she began to wonder if she was praying in the right direction. Was God taking them through this season of suffering to give them something He couldn't give them any other way? She knew God loved her daughter even more than she did. She knew His plans were to prosper her and not to harm her, to give her hope and a future. She also knew some good and godly people are not healed on this earth and that suffering is their ministry. So, she decided to dig deep into Jesus, to plunge to the depths of His love. She would open her heart and mind to the treasure found only in suffering.

Read Ecclesiastes 7:1,2.

¹A good name is better than precious ointment, and the day of death than the day of birth. ²It is better to go to the house of mourning than to go to the house of feasting for this is the end of all mankind, and the living will lay it to heart.

What is the value of a good name?

❋ Why do you think Solomon tells us the day of death is better than the day of birth?

❋ What can you learn at a funeral that you can't learn at a baby shower?

Read Ecclesiastes 7:3-6.

What are the paradoxes in verses 3, 4, and 5?

Under what conditions would those paradoxes be true?

At a funeral, we honor the name of the dear departed. We recount the ways that they created a name for themselves that blessed others. Having a good name, Solomon says, is better than having costly treasure. When we celebrate the end of a life with a memorial service, we cannot help but think about our own death. It brings us to a new perspective on how we are spending our own lives. Does it mean that you should never go to parties and always maintain a somber outlook? No! Solomon is just giving us some perspective from his point of view as someone at the end of his life.

Week 6: Day 1

Death, pain and suffering are subjects we don't usually embrace. It is difficult to face them and even harder to endure. The Covid-19 pandemic brought suffering to the whole world through loss of health, contact, income, opportunities and, in the worst cases, loss of life. Everyone living today has endured suffering from the coronavirus in some way. But pain and sorrow have been with us since we left Eden. So, how do we navigate a life that includes some seasons of misery? Solomon researches the topic for us and gives us his conclusion: Pain and suffering aren't all bad. They become master teachers to give us instruction that can't be gained any other way. They cause us to stop and evaluate our lives. No one on their deathbed is worried about making more money or buying new things. They aren't trying to climb any vocational or social ladders. They are the most concerned about love and relationships. So, Solomon tells us, "Sorrow is better than laughter" because it brings wisdom with it.

In Ecclesiastes 5 and 6, he said that money is over-rated, but in chapter 7 he teaches us that pain and suffering are greatly under-rated. Our sorrows can make us stronger; or we can allow them to embitter us as they dig our grave slowly. Why do some people respond to their troubles with anger and bitterness, rejecting God, while others pursue God in their trials with passion and maturity?

Read Romans 5:1-5.
¹Therefore, since we have been justified by faith, we have peace with God through our Lord Jesus Christ. ²Through him we have also obtained access by faith into this grace in which we stand, and we rejoice in hope of the glory of God. ³Not only that, but we rejoice in our sufferings, knowing that suffering produces endurance, ⁴and endurance produces character, and character produces hope, ⁵and hope does not put us to shame, because God's love has been poured into our hearts through the Holy Spirit who has been given to us.

Fill in the blank from verse 3:

Not only that, but we _____ in our _____ ,

knowing that suffering produces _____ .

Endurance produces _____

Character produces _____

Hope does not _____

Some things can only be obtained through suffering. Don't get me wrong. I hate suffering! Because our daughter suffered for over three years with a debilitating illness, and I can tell you, I suffered right along with her. I struggled with feelings of anger and despair as I watched her pain. I'm a mom, and I wanted to solve the problem; but I couldn't. I wanted to take the burden from her, but it was not mine to carry. I could only offer the ministry of intercession, comfort and practical help. I had to press in, hold on, and dig deep into the treasure that is Jesus and leave the rest up to Him. When I began writing this book, we were still in God's waiting room awaiting her healing.

Miraculously, she had a breakthrough that has brought her back to health. Through this experience, we have seen God's transformation, not only in her body, but also in our hearts and minds. He's shown us areas of our lives that needed His cleansing power. God didn't waste our sorrows, but used them to accomplish something that couldn't have been done any other way.

Read II Corinthians 1:5-7.
⁵For as we share abundantly in Christ's sufferings, so through Christ we share abundantly in comfort too. ⁶If we are afflicted, it is for your comfort and salvation; and if we are comforted, it is for your comfort, which you experience when you patiently endure the same sufferings that we suffer. ⁷Our hope for you is unshaken, for we know that as you share in our sufferings, you will also share in our comfort.

How does Paul connect suffering and comfort?

Did Paul have a life free of suffering?

Did Jesus have a life free of suffering?

Read Ephesians 3:13.
So I ask you not to lose heart over what I am suffering for you, which is your glory.

Paul understood our suffering because he experienced it himself. His suffering was being unjustly accused and imprisoned. But he turned his suffering into an opportunity for others to encounter God. His prayer is that his suffering wouldn't be in vain but would lead others to Christ.

Read Ecclesiastes 7:7-10.

What is the danger in verse 7?

What is the danger in verse 8?

What is the danger in verse 9?

What is the danger in verse 10?

In verse 7, Solomon sees that the first danger of oppression and suffering is that it might drive us to think irrationally. There is a temptation to blame someone or something for the pain, and we tend to find a scapegoat close at hand. Sometimes we lash out at those who are trying to help. So, we need to resist that lure that will take us off track. We need to do what Psalm 46:10 urges, "Be still and know that He is God." Stop the shame and blame game and quietly rest in the Father's hands.

- ♦ Take a moment to cease striving and be still in God's presence, bringing your suffering to Him.

In verse 8, Solomon says the second danger in suffering is impatience. Years of struggling with a health problem or years of struggle in a difficult marriage make it hard to keep going. But the waiting room is where God works best.

- Commit to sitting in God's waiting room until He calls your name.

The next danger of pain and suffering is that anger is another easy way to get off track with God's plan to redeem your sorrows. For some, one of the first emotions we feel when dealing with physical or emotional pain is fury. We rage, "Why did this happen?" We feel helpless and out of control. God doesn't mind hearing your angry outbursts, so pour them all out onto Him.

- Unburden your heart and tell God exactly how you feel. And when you're through, consciously receive His love and put your anger to rest.

Finally, in verse 10, Solomon is reminding us of how often we say, "But what about those good old days? It was so much better then!" Solomon tells us, "Forget that! What is past is past, and it needs to stay there. That was then. This is now. Embrace your present circumstances and ask God to give you wisdom and grace for today."

- Don't look back to the past. Keep moving forward to what God has for you ahead. It's a new normal. Grow in wisdom as you move into your future.

Read Ecclesiastes 7:10-14.

What is the advantage of wisdom when you are suffering?

Who can make straight what God has made crooked?

In the day of adversity, what should you consider?

Instead of railing against God when you find yourself in adversity, take His hand and walk in the direction of wisdom where He is walking. You may never understand your circumstances and why they were assigned to you, but as you trust the Lord and draw wisdom from His Word, He will take your suffering and use it for good.

Paul said it in Romans 8:28:
And we know that for those who love God all things work together for good, for those who are the called according to his purpose.

And in II Corinthians 4:16-18:
¹⁶So, we do not lose heart. Though our outer self is wasting away, our inner self is being renewed day by day. ¹⁷For this light momentary affliction is preparing for us an eternal weight of glory beyond all comparison, ¹⁸as we look not to the things that are seen but to the things that are unseen. For the things that are seen are transient, but the things that are unseen are eternal.

A Bit of Wisdom

If you find yourself going through a season of suffering, be kind and gentle to yourself. Don't expect too much because right now, you need process time to heal and sort through your jumbled emotions. The best way to do that is to go on a private retreat. Maybe you know a place where you can go to be completely alone and unplugged from electronics.

Take a blank notebook, several good pens, and your hard copy of the Bible. Bring your favorite worship music. If possible, stay for a day or two or even longer if you can. If that's not an option for you, just spend a few hours alone in your own bedroom. Allow God to comfort you, speak to you, and guide you. Give yourself permission to rest a lot, to completely unwind, and to sit in God's presence quietly. Ask Him to lead you into His Word to give you wisdom and direction.

I had such a "retreat" during two cases of Covid-19 and the recovery afterward. I spent many days alone in our bedroom, as I had to be isolated even from my own husband in our home. This solace was not one I would have asked for, but God used it to speak to me and to drive home the messages of this book. I can say from personal experience that suffering and solace can provide the space in your life for God to do a work that probably wouldn't happen any other way. I've learned not to fight it but to invite Him into my suffering and learn all I can at His feet.

The Balancing Act — Day 2

Lord, I love You, and I worship You. In You is all wisdom and knowledge. Please teach me the lessons of wisdom through Your Word that strengthen and encourage me. Forgive me when I act foolishly. Lead me in the way everlasting. In Jesus' name I pray. Amen.

As the middle child, Celina was both a peacemaker and a clown. When you wanted to have fun, she was the one to go to for the happy occasion. While a dedicated, sincere Christian, she wasn't starched and stuffy. She kept in balance when to be serious and when to be silly. She believed life should be crammed full of both in equal measure. She could stay up all night praying with a friend and a few days later stay up all night playing monopoly with her nieces and nephews. She was definitely the fun auntie. Everyone wanted to be with Celina. She gave powerful and moving speeches at her parent's funerals but afterwards, her house is where everyone wanted to gather to lighten the mood and share some laughter with the tears. Celina had discovered the joy of balancing the heavy things of life with the lighthearted.

One of the things wise Solomon learned in his search for weathering the Winter Season is to keep life in balance. It's easy during a time of hardship to fall out of balance in body, mind, and spirit. Wrong food, wrong thinking, and self-righteousness can send us over the edge. But the Teacher leads us to the truth that too much of anything is probably not a good thing. He brings us back into balance.

- **SPIRITUAL BALANCE**

Read Ecclesiastes 7:15-18.

Can you name an example of a person who fits Solomon's descriptions in verse 15?

✹ What does it mean to be "overly righteous" and "too wise?"

✹ What is Solomon's solution to being in balance?

Solomon is asking questions we have all asked: Why do the good die young and the evil, mean ones live long lives? This is something even Solomon's wisdom could not discern. Only God knows. But to avoid dying before your time, Solomon tells us to find the balance. He says to not be overly self-righteous and legalistic to the detriment of others and yourself. There have even been some who were zealous for God, thinking they were righteous in their actions, when in reality they put themselves in harm's way needlessly and suffered the consequences. I had an experience once that taught me to use wisdom, balance, and discretion even in taking on ministry assignments.

While we were living in Indonesia, I was asked to go to India to speak for a group of ladies near a jungle area. About 250 women registered for the event, and all was prepared. But about three weeks before my departure, my pastor's wife came to our home with alarming news. She had had a vivid dream that while I was speaking for the conference, I was attacked by a tiger and mauled in front of the women. She had had the same dream for several nights in a row. She asked me to pray and consider very carefully before I went to India. I had never had this experience before, but I was paying close attention. David and I prayed together that night, and he sensed we needed more prayer warriors to help us pray through to a decision. I gathered my prayer team in Jakarta of about 12 women who prayed with me for several hours every Monday. When I related the dream to them, at first, they said, "We'll just pray for your protection, and you'll be fine."

But we got out our Bibles and prayed for more than an hour. As we saw where God was leading us in His Word to pray, we all realized that the dream was His sign for me to stay home. While disappointed, the pastor understood when I explained the dream. He carried on with teaching the women.

A few days later he sent me an astonishing report. While he was teaching, riots broke out in that area against white people, and many were attacked and some were murdered. He said to me that he and the ladies praised God that I had listened to His warning. It was not a safe place for a tall, fair American woman to be at that time. Sometimes the most righteous thing to do is to stay home.

In verse 17 Solomon says extreme wickedness is even more foolhardy than extreme righteousness. A wicked lifestyle can lead to early death. We all know of young entertainers who met an untimely death through a drug overdose. What a foolish waste of life! The God-fearing person will avoid both the extremes of legalism and libertinism and lead a balanced life that is truly righteous and wise.

♦ EMOTIONAL BALANCE

Read Solomon's proverbs in Ecclesiastes 7:19-22 and write the main point of what you learn from each one.

¹⁹Wisdom gives strength to the wise man more than ten rulers who are in a city.

> Example: Wisdom makes you strong.

²⁰Surely there is not a righteous man on earth who does good and never sins.

>

²¹Do not take to heart all the things that people say, lest you hear your servant cursing you.

>

²²Your heart knows that many times you yourself have cursed others.

>

Solomon continues to call us into balance. If you are already wise, you're probably not as wise as you think you are. Be humble and keep gaining more wisdom. You're never finished learning. Be a life-long learner. If you are already a righteous, God-loving person, don't be shocked when you sin. You're probably not as righteous as you think you are. Don't beat yourself up. Confess your sins, receive Christ's forgiveness and move on. If you have a following and God has given you a flock to care for, you're probably not as popular as you think you are. Don't take to heart the negative things people say about you, Solomon warns us. You've cut down someone else before, so give grace to those who hurt you with criticism. Have a thick skin and a soft heart.

Read Ecclesiastes 7:23-25.

Did Solomon find ultimate wisdom?

Why wasn't he satisfied with the great wisdom God gave to him?

Solomon was searching for what he already had. God had given him all the wisdom he needed. He needed only to stop searching within himself and stop searching in the world "under the sun" and look up. The Apostle Paul explains where we can find ultimate wisdom.

Read I Corinthians 2:11-16.
^{11}For who knows a person's thoughts except the spirit of that person, which is in him? So also no one comprehends the thoughts of God except the Spirit of God. ^{12}Now we have received not the spirit of the world, but the Spirit who is from God, that we might understand the things freely given us by God. ^{13}And we impart this in words not taught by human wisdom but taught by the Spirit, interpreting spiritual truths to those who are spiritual. ^{14}The natural person does not accept the things of the Spirit of God, for they are folly to him, and he is not able to understand them because they are spiritually discerned. ^{15}The spiritual person judges all things, but is himself to be judged by no one. ^{16}"For who has understood the mind of the Lord so as to instruct him?" But we have the mind of Christ.

✹ How does God give us wisdom?

Paul understood that life "above the sun" is life in the Son, Jesus Christ. He would agree with Solomon that finding balance in our lives with wisdom is not easy to find. We cannot find it on our own. It comes by *inspiration*, not just *information*. It comes when we have an intimate relationship with Jesus Christ and are filled with the Holy Spirit. That is when we have the mind of Christ.

♦ PHYSICAL BALANCE

Now Solomon turns his attention to another area of his life where he is completely out of balance.

Read Ecclesiastes 7:26-28.
²⁶And I find something more bitter than death: the woman whose heart is snares and nets, and whose hands are fetters. He who pleases God escapes her, but the sinner is taken by her. ²⁷Behold, this is what I found, says the Preacher, while adding one thing to another to find the scheme of things— ²⁸which my soul has sought repeatedly, but I have not found. One man among a thousand I found, but a woman among all these I have not found.

What kind of woman is Solomon describing?

Why didn't he find a godly woman among his thousand women, including 700 wives and 300 concubines?

Solomon's sex life is completely out of balance and out of God's will. He had hundreds of women instead of one covenant wife. His heathen wives were responsible for leading Solomon away from worshiping the one, true God. To be clear, Solomon is speaking of wayward, sinful women. He's not speaking about women in general. We can choose which kind of woman we will be. We can use our feminine wiles to entrap a man, or we can use our God-given femininity to love and satisfy our husbands.

If you are not married, wait for a good and godly man, and then marry him before you enter into a sexual relationship. After you are married, stay faithful to your vows. If you're married, satisfy your husband's sexual needs and make your sex life a priority. You and your husband will both be less vulnerable to sexual sin if you are content with married love.

Now you can understand why it was important to Solomon to write **Proverbs 31:10-12.**

¹⁰An excellent wife who can find? She is far more precious than jewels. ¹¹The heart of her husband trusts in her, and he will have no lack of gain. ¹²She does him good, and not harm, all the days of her life.

A Bit of Wisdom

What kind of woman do you want to be? A Proverbs 31 woman or a Proverbs 7 woman? If you aren't married and want to be, spend time today in prayer asking God for a good man. Then trust Him to bring the right person into your life. If you are married, recommit yourself to honoring and respecting your husband and submitting to his authority. Bless him in some special way today.

Follow the Leader — Day 3

Lord Jesus, I humble myself before You today. Teach me to be open and vulnerable to all You want to reveal to me. Make me a woman whose life is lined up with Your own heart. I ask this in the name of Jesus. Amen.

Madeline and Luke loved living in Asia and serving the people God had called them to love, but being expatriates had its challenges. The local laws were confusing and to them, often senseless. The laws were not necessarily there to protect the people but to protect the sovereign's wealth. Sometimes the rules were unfair, especially to outsiders. But God spoke to them through His Word and in prayer that one of the greatest ways to give a testimony of their submission to God was to submit to the authority of the land where they lived.

Read Ecclesiastes 8:2-9.

✵ Who is the authority in this passage?

✵ Who are authorities in your life that you should be submitting to?

Solomon admonishes us to honor those in authority and submit accordingly. When King Saul was pursuing David in II Samuel 24, David had the opportunity to kill Saul in a cave where he was hiding. But David refused to let his men take Saul's life. He said in verse 6, *"The Lord forbid that I should do such a thing to my master, the Lord's anointed, or lift my hand against him, for he is anointed of the Lord."* Solomon is simply saying to us from Ecclesiastes 8:5, "If you want to stay out of trouble, follow the rules!"

Read Romans 13:1-4.

¹Let everyone be subject to the governing authorities, for there is no authority except that which God has established. The authorities that exist have been established by God. ²Consequently, whoever rebels against the authority is rebelling against what God has instituted, and those who do so will bring judgment on themselves. ³For rulers hold no terror for those who do right, but for those who do wrong. Do you want to be free from fear of the one in authority? Then do what is right and you will be commended. ⁴For the one in authority is God's servant for your good. But if you do wrong, be afraid, for RULERS do not bear the sword for no reason. They are God's servants, agents of wrath to bring punishment on the wrongdoer. (NIV)

Who establishes governing authorities?

Why should we submit to our governing authorities?

Our rulers are described by Paul as God's _____.

Submitting to authority is not something most of us cherish. In fact, our post-modern world rebels at the very thought of purposefully submitting to authority. But God has established authorities for our lives to bring order and give us peace. If you are married, God has established an order of authority for your home as well.

Read Ephesians 5:22-26, 33.

²²Wives, submit to your own husbands, as to the Lord. ²³For the husband is the head of the wife even as Christ is the head of the church, his body, and is himself its Savior. ²⁴Now as the church submits to Christ, so also wives should submit in everything to their husbands. ²⁵Husbands, love your wives, as Christ loved the church and gave himself up for her, ²⁶that he might sanctify her, having cleansed her by the washing of water with the word.

³³However, let each one of you love his wife as himself, and let the wife see that she respects her husband.

✺ What authority is a wife supposed to obey?

✺ Do all women have to obey all men?

✺ How will you put this passage into practice this week?

Women are not inferior and don't have to cower to all men. Married women submit to their own husband's authority, not losing their identities or their voices of influence, but supporting their husband's leadership role in their home with strength and commitment. God has given structure to our homes to bring order and peace. To bring this order, not only are wives supposed to submit to their husbands, but children should submit to the authority of their parents.

Read Ephesians 6:1-4.
¹Children, obey your parents in the Lord, for this is right. ²"Honor your father and mother" (this is the first commandment with a promise), ³"that it may go well with you and that you may live long in the land." ⁴Fathers, do not provoke your children to anger, but bring them up in the discipline and instruction of the Lord.

✺ Do you need to apologize to your children for giving them instructions to obey?

✺ What is the difference between children obeying their parents and children honoring their parents?

You don't need to apologize to your children for giving them instructions to obey. They are commanded by God's Word to obey your authority. But first, they need to know that you love them unconditionally. Children who know they are deeply loved can receive fair discipline. You must be very prayerful and careful about the rules you establish for your children. They should be fair, firm and lead them to strong, secure, godly lives of great character. They shouldn't cower in fear before you but should know for sure that each rule you lay down is to be obeyed because of your great love for them. Love is the motivation for establishing authority in your home.

As your children become adults the roles change, and they no longer submit to your authority. Now your role as parent is to be a counselor and friend. They are commanded to honor you, so give them every reason to show you respect. Act respectably! Show them by your example how to love those around you unconditionally. Teach them how to give financial resources with joy. Let them catch you praying, studying the Word, and teaching others to follow Jesus.

If you are a single adult woman, you are still under authority. While you are no longer under your parents' authority, you will be under the authority of your boss at work, showing respect and following their directives. If you can't do that in good conscience, you will want to find another job. If you are in ministry, you will submit to the one in charge. If you are in ministry on your own, you probably have a board of directors to answer to and if you don't, you should organize one. We all need to be accountable to someone.

Read Ecclesiastes 8:10-15.

If the "wicked" are those who disobey and defy authority and those who "fear God" are those who stay under authority, according to verses 12 and 13, what are the consequences of their actions?

According to Solomon, is life fair? Do those who stay under authority always get rewarded in this life?

✺ What is Solomon's recommendation to all of us in light of "life isn't fair"?

Read Ecclesiastes 8:15.

Solomon warns us that even if we stay under our authorities, sometimes in this life, we will be treated unfairly. My mother told me over and over throughout my life, "Honey, whoever told you that life was fair?" When I railed against an injustice, that was always her reply. Her recommendation lined up with Solomon's wisdom: Be joyful! Don't spend your energy on trying to make everything "fair" and getting even. Focus on fearing God, putting Him first in your life, then set your mind on enjoying the life you have. If you look for it, you can always find joy. Yes, there will always be those who get by with disobedience. Yes, there will even be those who look religious on the outside, but inside their hearts are full of sin. Yes, sometimes you will take punishment that should have gone to someone else. Everyone won't always follow the rules. But you can choose to stay under God's authority and the authorities He has placed over you. And you can choose JOY!

A Bit of Wisdom

Staying under your God-given authorities might be hard for you. If you're married, submitting to your husband's authority may be the last thing you want to do. I recommend starting in the area where you're experiencing the greatest conflict with your husband. Are you fighting over money? Then choose one area of your finances and let him lead. Demonstrate your submission to God and submission to your husband in that one small thing. As you begin to learn how to support his leadership, you can take the next step to another area of your marriage.

If you are single, try this same principle at work, at church, or in a community setting. If someone is in charge, and that someone isn't you, show them respect in a tangible way by submitting to their authority.

And when you've had success in that area, throw yourself a little party! Eat, drink and be merry!

The Final Graduation
Day 4

Lord Jesus, You told us that in this world we would have tribulation, but we thank You that You have overcome the world. Give us strength when we are weak, give us courage when we suffer, and give us Your life that is abundant and free. Lord, today please teach me how a believer faces their own mortality—without morbidity. I want to be full of joy even when contemplating the end of my life on earth. I know my days are all in Your hands. All the days ordained for me were written in Your book before one of them came to be. Show me how to walk in peace and joy as I finish my race. In Jesus' name I pray. Amen.

Elizabeth's lupus was advancing. The doctor had just informed her that dialysis was now necessary, and she knew the risk of infection. So, in her typical way, Elizabeth decided to face it all head on. Not one to shy away from difficulties, she began to put her house in order. Since Stephen's death, she knew something of what her children would face when she was gone. So, she began documenting all of her accounts, updating her will, and creating a file of her usernames and passwords, but she knew there was much more to be done. She wanted to live joyfully to the very last day.

She decided the best way to spend her energy and time with her limited physical ability would be to write a memoir for her grandchildren of the adventures she and Stephen had shared and to include family stories from generations gone by. The more she thought about it, the more excited she became about leaving a legacy of God-stories for her descendants. As she wrote, she prayed that the readers—grand and great-grandchildren she would probably never meet—would pick up the little book on just the right day at just the right time to make an impact on their lives for God's glory. Now she'd better get busy! She didn't know how much time God would allow her on this earth, and she wanted to finish strong.

She started slowly, but as more stories took shape, the words began to flow. She worked into the night on one particular story of God's amazing grace in their lives. The more she thought and prayed over each word, the deeper her thoughts ran. God inspired her to write in her introduction these words, "The more I know, the more I realize I don't understand much of anything. But this I do know: That I love you more than life itself and that my life can only be explained by God's miracles. This little book gives you a front row seat into your family history. Now it's your turn to add your chapter to the God-story of our family. Life is brief, and you want to make the most of it. I believe in you. You can do this. Love, Grandma."

Read Ecclesiastes 8:16, 17.

What is the limit of wisdom?

Solomon has used this phrase, "applied my heart" several times in this book. Solomon is not just seeking knowledge or academia. This is a deep seeking from his heart. Solomon probably wrote this book later in his life, after he had written Proverbs, after he had married 700 women (mostly political alliances) and had 300 concubines, and after he had built palaces and the Temple. He confessed that these experiences and his deep seeking of wisdom caused him to have sleepless nights. He finally realized no man can fully understand all of God's ways. The subject that troubled Solomon most is the subject of death. He began to grapple with end-of-life issues.

Read Ecclesiastes 9:1-6.

What is the same event that happens to everyone whether they are righteous or evil according to verses 2 and 3?

What should we take advantage of while we are living? (verses 4-6)

Solomon names the common destiny of us all, whether wise or foolish, good or bad. We will all experience death. But there is more.

Read Ecclesiastes 9:7-10.

⁷Go, eat your bread with joy, and drink your wine with a merry heart, for God has already approved what you do. ⁸Let your garments be always white. Let not oil be lacking on your head. ⁹Enjoy life with the wife whom you love, all the days of your vain life that he has given you under the sun, because that is your portion in life and in your toil at which you toil under the sun. ¹⁰Whatever your hand finds to do, do it with your might, for there is no work or thought or knowledge or wisdom in Sheol, to which you are going.

✺ What does Solomon continually encourage us to do in our time on earth?

What encouragement does he give for our marriages?

Fill in the blanks from verse 10:

Whatever your hand finds to do, do it _____ _____ _____, for there is no work or thought or knowledge or wisdom in Sheol, to which you are going.

After all of Solomon's deep thinking and contemplating, he arrives at a simple framework for life: Since we will all die, we should live life fully while we can! Solomon tells us to enjoy our food by enjoying a good meal. He tells us to enjoy our social life by taking off black mourning and sackcloth and wear white and rejoice.

He tells us to enjoy our marriage with sexual, social, and emotional intimacy because that is a gift from God. He tells us to enjoy our work, and it sounds like Paul quoted Solomon in Colossians 3:23, *"Whatever you do, work heartily, as for the Lord and not for men."* He tells us to take all of the gifts that God has given to us and to enjoy them by using them for His glory. Do what you do with excellence and unto the Lord. This is what brings true satisfaction. Jesus came to bring us abundant life (John 10:10b), and He meant for us to enjoy it.

So yes, life on earth can be difficult and someday will end. But we know the end of the story. Jesus has redeemed us, and someday we will live with Him in heaven. While we are still living in our earth suits, we have a choice as to how we live our lives. Solomon is saying to us, "Enjoy the gifts God has given you and stay close to Him, and you'll be living life at its best!"

A Bit of Wisdom

Take stock of how much you are enjoying your life:

Do you enjoy food? Are you making good food choices that make you feel better?

Do you enjoy your marriage? Are you spending quality time with your beloved, creating romantic interludes where you can connect spiritually, emotionally and physically? Are you actively working on problem areas in your communication to bring healing and wholeness to your union?

Do you enjoy your children and grandchildren? Are you spending one-on-one time with them in a way that makes you both happy?

Do you enjoy your home? Is it a haven of peace and rest or so cluttered you can't enjoy it? Do you enjoy your outdoor space, even if it's a small balcony at your apartment? What can you do this week to make your indoor and outdoor living spaces more enjoyable?

Life is to be enjoyed and savored. Have fun this week raising your "joy meter!"

How to Live Well in an Uncertain World
Day 5

Lord, we live in a fallen world, and we need You. Thank You for giving us Your Spirit and Your Word to guide us through the "mine fields" of life. Thank You for Your great love that never changes. We love You, Jesus. It is in Your name we pray. Amen.

Daphne's life sometimes felt heavy and relentless. No matter how much she planned, life often took a left turn that she didn't see coming. She had dreamed of retirement, thinking life would finally be free and easy; but when Richard left her, those plans went out the window. She'd need to work long after she was 65 to make ends meet. She had planned to spend her golden years with grandchildren all around her, only to suffer with one of her kids over infertility; and the one who did have children, took a job far away, taking her grandchildren with him. She thought she'd saved enough for her care in her elder years, only to see her savings dwindle too quickly. She had always thought she would celebrate a 50th wedding anniversary, but infidelity and divorce took away that possibility. Life had thrown her a curve ball, and she wondered if she could maintain hope.

When she called her pastor's wife, she knew the older woman would help her find answers to keep going. As they sat chatting over coffee and Daphne poured out the litany of injustices in her life, the woman across from her looked deeply into her eyes and spoke words she needed to hear. "Daphne, you're searching for hope and answers in the wrong place. You're looking at your circumstances, and I agree, they're pretty grim. You have a right to feel sad and even mad about some of these things. But you called me because you don't want to stay in that dark place. You're ready to walk out into the light and breathe. So, my dear, start by seeking God Himself and not just what He can do for you. Yes, you need help and you need answers, but first you just need Him. So, seek Him with all of your heart. Trust Him. Listen to Him. He'll show you how to take your next steps with great wisdom."

"Let's get out our Bibles and read Matthew 6:33. *'But seek first the kingdom of God and his righteousness, and all these things will be added to you.'* God knows everything you need, Daphne, and He'll supply it all. Let's also read James 1:5, 6, *'If any of you lacks wisdom, let him ask God, who gives generously to all without reproach, and it will be given him.'* I'm going to ask God to give you supernatural wisdom, like the wisdom He gave Solomon."

Read Ecclesiastes 9:11-16.

What are the injustices Solomon documents?

What are the two things that happen to everyone?

In his example, what does Solomon note as an antidote for injustice in life?

Solomon observes life as a scientist and sees injustice at its worst. He tells us that no matter how much you prepare for the future, when time and chance enter the picture, anything can happen. He doesn't answer the question of why life is the way that it is, but he does offer some temporal solutions for how to live this life. One of those solutions is wisdom.

In his example, Solomon sees a battle that looks like a lost cause. A little city is attacked by a great king who had siege works built up against the walls. "Siege works" were temporary fortresses built to allow the enemy army to not only shoot arrows and throw missiles of war down into the city, but also to allow them to scale ladders that lifted the soldiers over the walls. In a twist of the narrative, a poor but wise man delivered the city. Solomon is once again preaching the value of wisdom. In our own daily battles, it is a weapon in our arsenal to protect us.

Read Ecclesiastes 9:17, 18.
¹⁷The words of the wise heard in quiet are better than the shouting of a ruler among fools. ¹⁸Wisdom is better than weapons of war, but one sinner destroys much good.

✵ When are the words of a wise person better than those of a ruler?

Wisdom is better than _____.

Read Proverbs 2:1-11.
¹My son, if you receive my words and treasure up my commandments with you, ²making your ear attentive to wisdom and inclining your heart to understanding ³yes, if you call out for insight and raise your voice for understanding, ⁴if you seek it like silver and search for it as for hidden treasures, ⁵then you will understand the fear of the LORD and find the knowledge of God. ⁶For the LORD gives wisdom; from his mouth come knowledge and understanding; ⁷he stores up sound wisdom for the upright; he is a shield to those who walk in integrity, ⁸guarding the paths of justice and watching over the way of his saints. ⁹Then you will understand righteousness and justice and equity, every good path; ¹⁰for wisdom will come into your heart, and knowledge will be pleasant to your soul; ¹¹discretion will watch over you, understanding will guard you.

How do we obtain God's wisdom for ourselves?

What do we learn about God in verses 7 and 8?

What will happen to us when we obtain wisdom according to verses 10-11?

As we learned during the Covid-19 pandemic, the world is full of uncertainty. God's wisdom is what will carry us through whatever life brings. Solomon urges us to receive and treasure God's words and commandments. When things are swirling around us and life is difficult, it is time to go back to the fundamentals of our faith. Do the things you know to do: Spend time reading and meditating on God's Word, spend time praying alone on your knees and also time praying in a group of at least two or three, give offerings from your financial resources to your local church and chose a type of fast that will help you focus on Christ alone.

A wise person makes life simpler when things are complicated. When you put Matthew 6 into practice, you'll find your balance during turbulence and your calm in the storm.

A Bit of Wisdom

You might want to create a family cookbook from recipes gathered from the older generation in your extended family. Think of it as an heirloom to pass down to your children and grandchildren. Make one page for each recipe including the signature dish, a picture of the cook, a bit about their life, and a wise saying from them. Print the pages and place them in a notebook with page protectors to keep the recipes clean. This treasure of family history can be given to the next generation who love to cook.

BIBLE STUDY NOTES

WEEK 7
WHAT BRINGS ULTIMATE MEANING TO LIFE?

A Personal Message to You from Solomon

This life is a series of decisions that will make an impact on you and those who are following you, whether you choose to go to the right by walking in the light or go to the left by walking in darkness. Go in the way you know you must go. That is where joy and peace lie. I took the other road and lived to regret it all my days. But in the end, I found the answer to having a life worth living. It is profound yet simple and it's available to every person. I will close my sermon with this message.

The Fly in the Ointment

Day 1

Lord, please give me the wisdom of Solomon to avoid the calamities of life and to trust in Your wisdom. Father, please, shine Your light into my life, revealing dark areas that need cleansing, healing, and Your redeeming grace. Since I live in a world of temptation and foolishness, please take off my blinders so I can see the truth about myself and walk in obedience to You. Do this work in me, I pray. In Jesus' name, Amen.

Abigail and Daphne's friend Rachel had lived next door to their parents for many years. She had been more like a sister than a friend. They had just celebrated her 73rd birthday together. Only a few days later, Abigail got the call from the hospital that Rachel had had a heart attack and didn't survive. How was it possible that their friend was gone so soon? Rachel had been a widow for a long time and never had children. In her will, she had left everything to the Page family who had befriended her for so many years. So, with heavy hearts and on top of all their other commitments, Abigail and Daphne began to clean out their neighbor's house.

The sisters knew their friend had a lot of "stuff" stored in the house after living there for more than 40 years, but what they found completely shocked and dismayed them. This wonderful lady, whom they trusted to be upright in every way, had credit cards that were charged to the limit and closets and closets full of out-of-date clothing and things she didn't need. This was a hidden part of her world that was unknown to her neighbors. Their loveable, cheerful neighbor had been only paying the smallest amount on each credit card, and now thousands and thousands of dollars were owed on the balances. Her reputation while she was living was absolutely spotless, and the sisters would do nothing to spoil her good name. But they were horrified at her reckless spending. How had this area of their friend's life remained in darkness? How could such a God-fearing woman have such glaring foolishness in her life?

Read Ecclesiastes 10:1, 2.

What outweighs wisdom and honor?

Solomon knew by personal experience that you can be the wisest man on earth and make a foolish choice that ruins your life. He chose the wrong path, and he knew the agony of life as a fool. God blessed him beyond measure with wisdom and wealth, but he chose the life and consequences of folly in his later years. He did what God had expressly told the kings of Israel not to do. He knew God's laws about marriage, especially to foreign, heathen wives; but he broke those laws anyway.

Read I Kings 11:1-10.

¹Now King Solomon loved many foreign women, along with the daughter of Pharaoh: Moabite, Ammonite, Edomite, Sidonian, and Hittite women, ²from the nations concerning which the LORD had said to the people of Israel, "You shall not enter into marriage with them, neither shall they with you, for surely they will turn away your heart after their gods." Solomon clung to these in love. ³He had 700 wives, who were princesses, and 300 concubines. And his wives turned away his heart. ⁴For when Solomon was old his wives turned away his heart after other gods, and his heart was not wholly true to the LORD his God, as was the heart of David his father.

⁵For Solomon went after Ashtoreth the goddess of the Sidonians, and after Milcom the abomination of the Ammonites. ⁶So Solomon did what was evil in the sight of the LORD and did not wholly follow the LORD, as David his father had done. ⁷Then Solomon built a high place for Chemosh the abomination of Moab, and for Molech the abomination of the Ammonites, on the mountain east of Jerusalem. ⁸And so he did for all his foreign wives, who made offerings and sacrificed to their gods. ⁹And the LORD was angry with Solomon, because his heart had turned away from the LORD, the God of Israel, who had appeared to him twice ¹⁰and had commanded him concerning this thing, that he should not go after other gods. But he did not keep what the LORD commanded.

✳ According to verse 2, why did God tell the Israelites not to marry foreign women?

✳ According to verses 4 and 5, when he was older something happened to Solomon's heart. What was that and why?

Solomon was a half-hearted follower of God. He started so well but ended his life in vanity and misery. No wonder there is such a difference in the way he wrote Proverbs and Song of Solomon and the tone of Ecclesiastes. Those who are faithful to God don't characterize life as meaningless, no matter what the circumstances. Solomon's life was vanity because he left his first love, and the wisest man who ever lived became a fool.

Like a dead fly that pollutes expensive perfume, a little bit of foolishness can ruin a life. A minister can be so effective in his ministry but have one inappropriate encounter with a woman that destroys his reputation and his family. A mother can sacrifice for her children and spend every waking moment in their care but scar them for life with a harsh, calloused, stinging comment. A college freshman can enter the university on a full academic scholarship and throw it all away by partying one night. A person can build a career with hard work and determination, only to see it all crumble with one stubborn, rebellious act against the boss. A neighbor can build a deep friendship with a neighbor for years and with one fight over a relatively small grievance lose the entire relationship. And the list goes on.

Dr. Garry Nation, author of *Fool: Identifying and Overcoming Character Deficiency Syndrome*, describes fools in four stages that spiral down. A first-degree fool, as Dr. Nation describes him, is a fool who makes dumb choices that get him into trouble. The Bible calls him "a simple fool," not because he isn't smart but because he is willfully disobedient to his own hurt. If a first-degree fool follows his passions unchecked, he will eventually descend to a second-degree fool. This self-confident, swaggering fool is arrogant as he flouts authority.

He strides into disobedience, believing he will never face the consequences of his actions. He is confident he can direct his own life without obeying God. If the second-degree fool continues in this prideful distain for right moral choices, he will drop to the level of the third-degree fool, the committed fool, who considers himself competent to construct his own right and wrong with his mind closed to any other opinion. He has rejected wisdom and made a commitment to destructive, foolish behavior. He is belligerent and contentious. The final stage is the fourth-degree fool, the "scorner." This wicked fool has gone a step further down to declare that he not only doesn't believe in God but that God is the enemy. He has a total contempt for the truth. He ridicules godliness, moral righteousness, and everything sacred.

In a nutshell, the simple fool doesn't realize his sinful choices have consequences, the self-confident fool doesn't believe sin has consequences, and the committed fool doesn't care if sin has consequences. But the scorner takes it a step further. This fool has not only rejected the intellectual idea of God but, having had some encounter with God, purposely refuses and rejects the Holy Spirit that has been revealed to him. This is the terminal fool.[1]

Solomon looks back on his life and tells us not to follow his foolish example. He points us to wisdom by telling us some things to watch for in life. In Ecclesiastes 10:2, he tells us the first way to avoid foolishness is to watch our HEARTS. The heart is where our passions, our dreams and our desires exist. It's the essence of who we are. If your heart is set on Jesus and His kingdom and if it is full of God's wisdom, your heart will direct you by God's Spirit to the right path. But if you are consumed with your own desires, of pleasing the flesh and your selfishness, and ignore God's way and His Word, your heart will be darkened by sin; and it will lead you in the wrong direction.

Are you on the right path?

Read Ecclesiastes 10:3-7.

Who recognizes a fool?

How does Solomon counsel us to relate to our authorities?

Where would Solomon see "folly set in high places" and the "rich sitting in a low place?"

In verse 3, Solomon says another way to avoid foolishness is to watch our STEPS. When a foolish person enters a room or walks down the street, everyone knows he's foolish except the fool! But a wise man watches his step, especially with someone in authority over you. If your superior challenges you, you have a choice. The foolish choice is to fire back reactive words that escalate division and destruction. But the wise choice is to act calmly and "let it go" to diffuse the situation. Of course, there are times to take a stand; but more often than not, it's best to stay calm, cool, and collected with your authorities, even when they are acting like a fool.

Read Ecclesiastes 10:8-11.

What are the consequences of sin in verse 8?

From what you know of Solomon's life, who quarried stones and who split logs?

Why do you think that would have caused hurt and danger?

How do you think Solomon is now feeling about all of his building projects?

Solomon describes the consequences of making foolish decisions and gives two examples. First, he says, if you dig a pit and then fall into it, you deserve to get hurt. Also, if you break through a "wall" or law, and a "snake" (the consequences) bites you, you deserve the pain. But sometimes you get hurt by doing the right thing. His examples of this are in his building projects. Men in the rock quarries and logging sites were hurt by working hard. Solomon may have been asking himself, "Was it really necessary to make those buildings so elaborate that someone would lose their life over it? Was it folly?"

Solomon tells us we need to avoid foolishness by watching our HEARTS, watching our STEPS, and now watching our WORDS…

Read Ecclesiastes 10: 12-14.

What do the wise man's words accomplish?

What characterizes the words of the foolish man?

✸ When have you experienced saying the wrong thing at the wrong time? How did it make you and those around you feel?

✸ When have you experienced saying the right thing at the right time? How did it make you and those around you feel?

> Write out a three-sentence prayer about your words.

Solomon knows the importance of words and speech. In his book of Proverbs, especially Proverbs 15, he preaches about the importance of words and how they are used.

Read Proverbs 15:1-7.
¹A soft answer turns away wrath, but a harsh word stirs up anger. ²The tongue of the wise commends knowledge, but the mouths of fools pour out folly. ³The eyes of the LORD are in every place, keeping watch on the evil and the good. ⁴A gentle tongue is a tree of life, but perverseness in it breaks the spirit. ⁵A fool despises his father's instruction, but whoever heeds reproof is prudent. ⁶In the house of the righteous there is much treasure, but trouble befalls the income of the wicked. ⁷The lips of the wise spread knowledge; not so the hearts of fools.

Solomon experienced both speaking in wisdom and speaking as a fool. He describes a fool's words as endless chatter. Solomon tells us we need to avoid foolishness by watching our HEARTS, watching our STEPS, watching our WORDS and now watching our JUDGMENTS.[2]

Read Ecclesiastes 10:16-20.

What did the kings and nobles do wrong in this passage?

Even if your ruler is acting foolishly, how are you instructed NOT to speak about them?

✺ How might this instruction help you in deciding how to use social media to air your opinions? How can you be wise with your words and still speak up for justice appropriately?

To avoid further foolishness, we must watch our judgments—especially in the political realm. If you live in a nation that elects officials, you should vote for those who are sober, not feasting and drinking in the morning and those who are diligent, hard workers and not slothful. You need to choose wise leaders who will work for the good of their people. There is a time for feasting, enjoying food and laughter, and there is a time for soberness. Choose leaders who use wisdom in their judgments.

Solomon is warning us about foolishness. Watch your heart. Watch your steps. Watch your words. Watch your judgments. We live in a foolish world, but God will give you wisdom for the journey when you ask, seek and knock for it.

Read I Corinthians 1:27-30.

²⁷But God chose what is foolish in the world to shame the wise; God chose what is weak in the world to shame the strong; ²⁸God chose what is low and despised in the world, even things that are not, to bring to nothing things that are, ²⁹so that no human being might boast in the presence of God. ³⁰And because of him you are in Christ Jesus, who became to us wisdom from God, righteousness and sanctification and redemption.

The enemy uses the foolishness of the world to try to distract and lead us away from the truth and wisdom of God through Jesus Christ. Solomon is God's messenger to warn us to beware and alert to the schemes of the enemy. Don't be a fool!

[1] *Fool: Identifying & Overcoming Character Deficiency Syndrome: A Biblical Investigation of Wisdom V. Folly,* by Garry Nation, Tate Publishing, 2006.

[2] Scot Pollok, Senior Pastor of Faith Bible Church, The Woodlands, TX, "Why?" sermon series, 2019.

A Bit of Wisdom

Many of you reading this book were born before the internet was developed. Social media is a relatively new phenomenon that our grandparents couldn't have fathomed. While Facebook, Instagram, and other social media outlets have connected the world via instant communication, it has also provided a platform for everyone to give their opinions—even when they shouldn't be shared. Be wise; think and pray before you post. Make sure your words are uplifting. Be honest, but edit your thoughts before they explode onto your social media page.

BIBLE STUDY NOTES

Generous Givers — Day 2

Lord, thank You for being so generous to me. Now teach me to open my heart and give to others. I ask You to speak to me about areas where I can share more of my resources. Speak clearly so I can obey and follow Your voice. I love You, Lord. In Jesus' name, Amen.

CELINA AND PAUL were a happy-go-lucky couple who loved to travel, loved to shop, and loved to eat at expensive restaurants. It was hard to keep up the lifestyle they had chosen, but with credit cards in hand, they happily charged away. While they were faithful in attendance at church, they never seemed to have enough to put into the offering plate as it was passed each Sunday. It was the most uncomfortable part of the service for them, and they were both glad when the plates had been collected and taken away.

One particular Sunday, the pastor was preaching on generosity. They both sat through the service staring at their expensive shoes. When they got into the car after church, they sat silently for a few minutes. Paul, turned to Celina with tears in his eyes. "That sermon got me. Celina, we can't keep on living like this. It's not right to spend everything on ourselves and have nothing to share. I want to start tithing with my next paycheck. It's going to be a radical change for us, but I know in my heart it's right to give the first 10 percent back to the Lord from our income and live on the 90 percent of God's blessings to us. And I want to start sharing some of the 90 percent, too. Our next-door neighbors have been out of work for six months, and I know they need help with groceries. Honey, are you with me?" Celina's lip trembled as she turned her large eyes on her husband's face. "Yes, Paul," she said quietly. "It's going to be tough, but I'm with you."

Read Ecclesiastes 11:1, 2.

¹Cast your bread upon the waters, for you will find it after many days. ²Give a portion to seven, or even to eight, for you know not what disaster may happen on earth.

※ If "your bread" is your own financial resource, what do you think it means to "cast your bread upon the waters" when you read it in context of the next verse?

How is verse 2 telling you to invest in treasure that is not on the earth?

Is there someone who comes to your mind to whom you would be able to help financially?

Solomon encourages us to send our financial resources out into the world to supply the needs of others. Since wealth is fickle and could be gone at any time with the whims of the marketplace, we should give generously now. Your return may or may not be financial but will return blessings and fulfillment when given with a genuine, generous heart.

One time, God impressed upon David and me that we should give away something that was very precious to us and represented some financial security. It was a hard decision; but once we made up our minds to give it, there were tears of joy and relief, knowing and sensing the Lord's presence and His blessing on our gift. That act of obedience was a catalyst for a big step of spiritual growth for us. It began our understanding of an important principle: You can't out-give God! Malachi 3:10 says, *"Bring the full tithe into the storehouse, that there may be food in my house. And thereby put me to the test, says the Lord of hosts, if I will not open the windows of heaven for you and pour down for you a blessing until there is no more need."*

Read Ecclesiastes 11:3, 4.

How are rain clouds generous?

How is a fallen tree generous to the land it falls upon?

What excuse for stinginess does the ungenerous man use in verse 4?

Solomon gives two examples of generosity and two examples of stingy selfishness. He says even rain clouds generously pour out their rain upon the earth and a fallen tree lies where it provides for those that find it. The stingy man looks for every excuse not to invest in others. He fearfully looks at what might happen in the future and doesn't give generously today.

Read Ecclesiastes 11:5, 6.

What does Solomon compare in verse 5?

What does Solomon tell us that we do not know, according to verse 6?

Solomon reminds us that we don't know how God's Spirit will work through the gifts we sow into the lives of others. That is up to Him alone. So, it is our job to sow generously our material wealth, our unconditional love, and the good news of Jesus Christ. We sow these gifts in the "morning" season of life when we are young and in the "evening" season when we are older.

Read Mark 4:3-8.

³"Listen! Behold, a sower went out to sow. ⁴And as he sowed, some seed fell along the path, and the birds came and devoured it. ⁵Other seed fell on rocky ground, where it did not have much soil, and immediately it sprang up, since it had no depth of soil. ⁶And when the sun rose, it was scorched, and since it had no root, it withered away. ⁷Other seed fell among thorns, and the thorns grew up and choked it, and it yielded no grain. ⁸And other seeds fell into good soil and produced grain, growing up and increasing and yielding thirtyfold and sixtyfold and a hundredfold."

As you sow your seed generously, pray to the Lord of the harvest that it will fall on good soil and bring forth 30, 60 or 100-fold!

A Bit of Wisdom

Giving is a skill that gets easier with practice. If you aren't giving to your local church, that's a good place to start. From there, ask the Lord to bring to you those who genuinely need your help and the encouragement of your support. Is there a recent disaster in any part of your country? Find a trusted local church in that area where you can send a donation or volunteer to help. Ask God to show you how to give "not too much and not too little."

BIBLE STUDY NOTES

Keeping the Past in the Past

Day 3

Lord Jesus, You created me in Your image, and I want to reflect Your glory. There is no God like You in heaven or on earth. You are the Almighty God, the Everlasting Father, the Prince of Peace. I worship You. Lord, I want to use all my days to reflect Your love and grace to all those around me. I commit my days to serve You and to complete the kingdom purposes You have for me. Give me the strength to finish well. In Jesus' name, Amen.

One of Elizabeth's constant prayers in this Winter Season of life was to finish strong and to hear Jesus say at the end of her life, "Well done, thou good and faithful servant." She longed to use her final days to be as effective, efficient, and productive as possible for God's kingdom. With advanced lupus, there was not a lot she could do now physically for anyone. But her spirit was strong and her prayer life more effective than ever. She poured over Scriptures to use as the basis for her prayers, knowing that God loves to bring to pass those things in His Word. She wanted to take advantage of these days while she still had enough brainpower and eyesight to intercede for her children and grandchildren, her pastor, her church, and the many missionaries she fervently prayed for each day. With her big, worn Bible in her feeble hands, Elizabeth went to work, calling on her beloved Savior to accomplish His will in each life.

Read Ecclesiastes 11:7, 8.

⁷Light is sweet, and it is pleasant for the eyes to see the sun. ⁸So if a person lives many years, let him rejoice in them all; but let him remember that the days of darkness will be many. All that comes is vanity.

✷ What is Solomon's advice to senior citizens of advanced age?

Why is Solomon contrasting light and darkness as it refers to older people?

As he begins to wrap up his sermon in Ecclesiastes, Solomon speaks to senior adults. He urges us to take advantage of the days of sunshine now and to rejoice always. The days of darkness are coming when our physical eyesight dims and our mental and physical acuity is weak. The wise person looks at the future and realizes that time is short and is of the essence. We must make the most of every single day and not waste the precious gift of time.

The New England Journal of Medicine in 2018 conducted a study to answer this question: What is the most productive decade of a person's life? The answer was between ages 60 and 70! Why? The children are grown and, with an empty nest, there is more available time and money. Life is easier in many ways. We have made most of our foolish mistakes by then and ideally, we are wiser.

In contrast to the old man, Solomon now turns to the youth.

Read Ecclesiastes 11: 9, 10.
⁹Rejoice, O young man, in your youth, and let your heart cheer you in the days of your youth. Walk in the ways of your heart and the sight of your eyes. But know that for all these things God will bring you into judgment. ¹⁰Remove vexation from your heart, and put away pain from your body, for youth and the dawn of life are vanity.

✷ What is Solomon's advice to the younger generation?

The beginning of verse 9 sounds like really bad parenting advice! Not many parents would say to their teenager, "Here are the car keys and a map. Go and do whatever your heart and eyes desire." That sounds crazy! But look at the end of verse 9, "But know that for all these things God will bring you into judgment." Our typical advice to young people is to say, "Be careful… there is a cruel, dark world out there." But Solomon's advice is better. "Enjoy life, but stay on the path of righteousness, purity, and godliness."

Solomon points out how fleeting youth is and that the young should refrain from any conduct that causes "vexation" or sorrows that might result from youthful lusts. Unfortunately, some of us made poor decisions in our youth that still cause pain and remorse in our later years. Don't pretend it's not there. We need to be honest with ourselves and honest with God to be freed from our past.

Our sinful past may only be between us and God, or it might involve others. It is important that we deal with this in the right way. If there is real guilt, there will be a specific conviction from the Holy Spirit. We need to pray like David in Psalms 139.

Read Psalm 139:23, 24.
²³Search me, O God, and know my heart; test me and know my anxious thoughts. ²⁴And see if there is any offensive way in me, and lead me in the way everlasting.

What is David's attitude toward God in these verses?

Write this prayer in your own words.

Once we know we have sinned, we need to confess it to God and receive His forgiveness. Unconfessed sin doesn't break relationship, but it does break fellowship and can cause us physical and emotional pain.

David experienced this as he explains in Psalms 32:3, 4, *"For when I kept silent, my bones wasted away through my groaning all day long. ⁴For day and night your hand was heavy upon me; my strength was dried up as by the heat of summer."* But in the same Psalm in verses 1-2, David describes the blessing of confessed sins, *"Blessed is the one whose transgression is forgiven, whose sin is covered. ²Blessed is the man against whom the LORD counts no iniquity, and in whose spirit there is no deceit."* Confessed sin brings healing and cleansing. I John 1:9 says, *"If we confess our sins, he is faithful and just to forgive us our sins and to cleanse us from all unrighteousness."*

- When have you experienced God's forgiveness, and what was the result in your life?

Sometimes the guilt you feel from the past might be false guilt. When you sense a dark cloud over you and you have a guilty feeling about everything, this can be a scheme of the enemy to attack your true identity in Christ and to defeat you as a child of God, making you feel guilty when, in fact, you aren't. This can happen in your youth or when you are a senior adult. But if you belong to Jesus, if God is your heavenly Father and you've accepted His son as Savior, you are not under judgment. Jesus took the punishment for your sins and mine, and they are paid for in full. Satan (the enemy) is the one condemned. John 12:47 says, *"If anyone hears my words and does not keep them, I do not judge him; for I did not come to judge the world but to save the world."* And Paul says in Romans 8:1, *"There is therefore now no condemnation for those who are in Christ Jesus."*

- Take time to examine your heart to see if there is an area where you are feeling false guilt and condemnation. Fully receive Christ's love and grace.

Sometimes our past memories involve hurt from others and the pain they have caused us. As we have been forgiven much by God, so we must be willing to forgive others. Jesus taught this in the Lord's Prayer and in Matthew 6:12, 14, 15, *"and forgive us our debts, as we also have forgiven our debtors. For if you forgive others their trespasses, your Heavenly Father will also forgive you, but if you do not forgive others their trespasses, neither will your Father forgive your trespasses."*

- Stop and think about past hurts and ask yourself: Have I totally forgiven their sin against me?

If you don't deal with the past, forgiving those who hurt you, the enemy can use it against you. Bitterness in your heart will fester and take you down. You will be free when you set others free. Jesus paid it all both for them and for you. Receive His forgiveness and grace and pass it on.

So, confess your sins, forgive others who have hurt you and walk in your true identity in Christ. Keep yourself free from the past and enjoy life fully in the present to get the most from your Winter Season.

A Bit of Wisdom

If you have teenagers or teenaged grandchildren, take them out to dinner one evening and talk about the principle behind these verses. Tell them how much you love them and want them to enjoy their lives. Inform them of the dangers lurking to trap youths and let them know you are praying daily for them. Keep in contact with them by texting loving and affirming messages.

The End of Days — Day 4

Lord Jesus, each year, each day, each moment is precious. Thank You for giving me life and for the time I have been given on this earth. Now, Lord, I want to really live my life fully before I die. Please, give me the grace to finish strong. Show me how to pass the baton to the next generation with humility and grace, with effectiveness and efficiency, and with wisdom as I pass blessings on to them. Lord, here I am. Use me to the very last day before I meet You. In Jesus' name, Amen.

ABIGAIL was approaching her 70th birthday, and this year new aches and pains were part of her daily life. She'd always been so strong and capable, such a tower of strength for her family; but she was really feeling her age today. Her back hurt, her feet hurt, and she had to take a little nap in the afternoon to make it through the day. She didn't like these restrictions. She had things to do! What bothered her most was not being able to help her kids with their kids. She loved her many grandchildren and could spend every day with them. But the lifting and running and stooping required for their care was just too much for her for long periods of time. She thoroughly enjoyed them for a few hours, but then she needed to rest.

She was thankful that she had spent her youth in service to God. Up until this year, she'd worked with children and young people at her church, pouring her life into theirs. She'd seen them develop and grow, and many were now in full-time ministry. Now, her main ministry was prayer and financial support for those young enough and with enough energy to keep up with the teenagers. She also spent times serving senior adults, both those who could still attend church and those who were confined to home. She called those who could hear her voice and prayed with them over the phone. She would serve her Lord as long as she had breath in her body. It's the way she wanted to finish her race.

Read Ecclesiastes 12:1.
Remember also your Creator in the days of your youth, before the evil days come and the years draw near of which you will say, "I have no pleasure in them."

Solomon mentions two kinds of "days" in the verse above? Name those two "days" in a person's life.

In chapter 12, Solomon turns his thoughts to the aging process as he concludes his book. He begins by saying, "Remember, you are God's creation; so serve Him from the start of your years and don't wait until the end of your life, when your strength is gone." Most of those who come to Christ accept Him before age 16. We know that we need to reach children and youth for Christ because the older one gets, hearts become harder.

Read Ecclesiastes 12:2, 3.
²before the sun and the light and the moon and the stars are darkened and the clouds return after the rain, ³in the day when the keepers of the house tremble, and the strong men are bent, and the grinders cease because they are few, and those who look through the windows are dimmed.

What would have to happen to your eyes for the natural light to be darkened?

What would have to happen to your mind for it to be cloudy?

What would have to happen to your arms ("keepers of the house") for you to tremble and for your back ("strong men") to be bent?

Week 7: Day 4

What would have to happen to your teeth ("grinders") to no longer be able to chew because they're falling out?

Who stands at the window looking out on the world with dimmed eyes?

The time will come, if you live long enough, when your body will age and there will be significant changes. You will probably lose the sharpness of both your eyesight and your mind. When one cloud of disability rolls past, another comes, just like clouds that come in again right after a rainstorm. Your mind will possibly become darkened and cloudy through the aging process, and there may come a time when you don't know the name of your spouse or your children. Alzheimer's and dementia can take not only our future but our past; or you might have a disease that causes trembling, like Parkinson's, when the "keepers of the house" (your arms and legs), begin to shake. You might suffer from arthritis when the "strong men are bent." The "grinders cease because they are few" represents our teeth that are being worn down and lost with age. All of these difficult things are symptoms of the body breaking down as we age.

When a person gets older and he stops going to work every day, he may stay at home and stand at the window looking out, contemplating his past life. Or he might live in a nursing home where his only view of the world is sitting by the window in the front lobby. Life is fading and is not as bright as it was in his youth. Inside every older person is a young person saying, "What happened?!" This is life and the way it is, and Solomon is saying to young people, "Remember your Creator NOW… before this time begins."

We don't need to live in denial, pretending old age won't happen to us or that it isn't happening now, but we need to love and accept our fragile bodies as they are. It's not a time to lose hope. It's a time to live fully with every day we have left.

Read Ecclesiastes 12:4, 5.

⁴and the doors on the street are shut—when the sound of the grinding is low, and one rises up at the sound of a bird, and all the daughters of song are brought low—⁵they are afraid also of what is high, and terrors are in the way; the almond tree blossoms, the grasshopper drags itself along, and desire fails, because man is going to his eternal home, and the mourners go about the streets—

If the "doors of the street" represent going out into the world, what is Solomon saying about them as you age?

If normal sounds are "low," what is Solomon saying about your hearing as you age?

Why would you get up at the slightest sound, like the sound of a bird, as you age?

Why would music be hard to hear as you age?

Why does climbing a tall height scare the aged?

How does a grasshopper usually get from place to place? What is he doing in Solomon's word picture?

What does it mean that "desire fails" in older people?

Where is our true "home?"

Solomon tells us the "doors on the street are shut" when we age as we tend to stay at home with loss of health and mobility. The "sound of grinding is low" refers to hearing loss as we age. "Rise up at the sound of a bird" indicates light or intermittent sleep in later life. The "daughters of song are brought low" represent the ear and voice that once loved music. The sounds that go with normal life are not as loud and distinct, because our hearing has gone. Remember your Creator before all this happens.

Solomon is saying with age we tend to be afraid of heights and falling because we might break a bone. We don't mend as quickly, and we are not as strong or as confident as we were in our youth. The almond tree turns from pink to white when the season is over and describes an old head with white hair. And then the wind comes and blows the blossoms away… just like some lose their hair completely. Since a grasshopper normally hops great distances, "the grasshopper drags itself along" is a picture of the lack of mobility with aging. "And desire fails," speaks of the lusts of youth, both of food and of sex, which fade away with age. Why do our bodies break down? Because man is going to his eternal home.

Read Isaiah 46:4.
Even to your old age and gray hairs I am he, I am he who will sustain you. I have made you and I will carry you; I will sustain you and I will rescue you.

Who will carry you through the aging process?

What do you have to be worried about?

God will carry you through the aging process. You don't have to be worried about the future. It's true that you won't get to skip out on death. You'll keep that divine and eternal appointment. You will either go to your eternal home in heaven, or you'll spend eternity in hell. It's your choice. If you accept Jesus Christ as your Lord and Savior from sin, if you ask Him to forgive your sins and cover them with His blood sacrifice on the Cross, you will be saved for all eternity and will be able to live with Him in the paradise of heaven. But if you do not accept Him personally, if you think your good works will buy you a ticket into heaven, you have doomed yourself to eternal hell. Your sins must be paid for in full. Either you will pay for them yourself with your own life forever condemned, or you will have them paid for you by the blood of Jesus Christ who died to pay for the sins of all men. Before you die, that choice will be made.

Read Matthew 25:31-34, 41, 46.

³¹"When the Son of Man comes in his glory, and all the angels with him, then he will sit on his glorious throne. ³²Before him will be gathered all the nations, and he will separate people one from another as a shepherd separates the sheep from the goats. ³³And he will place the sheep on his right, but the goats on the left. ³⁴Then the King will say to those on his right, 'Come, you who are blessed by my Father, inherit the kingdom prepared for you from the foundation of the world.

⁴¹"Then he will say to those on his left, 'Depart from me, you cursed, into the eternal fire prepared for the devil and his angels.

⁴⁶And these will go away into eternal punishment, but the righteous into eternal life."

Who are the sheep in this passage, and who are the goats?

What happens to the sheep?

What happens to the goats?

Who do you need to tell about Jesus and His love? Can you do that today? Pray for an opportunity to share the way of life with them.

Our funerals are coming. Mourners will come, but after the funeral they go back out into the streets. Solomon is saying, "You will go to your eternal home, and everyone else goes back to work!" We must remember our Creator now while there is still daylight. The "evil day" is coming when there will be no more time to choose Him. No more time to have our sins forgiven. For either we will die or we will be so old, with a mind that cannot comprehend His loving sacrifice for us, that time will run out.

Read Ecclesiastes 12:6-8.
⁶before the silver cord is snapped, or the golden bowl is broken, or the pitcher is shattered at the fountain, or the wheel broken at the cistern, ⁷and the dust returns to the earth as it was, and the spirit returns to God who gave it. ⁸Vanity of vanities, says the Preacher; all is vanity.

At birth, our souls and our bodies are bound together beautifully with a silver cord of life. Our bodies are connected by a heavenly umbilical cord to soul and spirit that gives us the capacity on this earth for relationship with God, but at death, the silver cord that held soul and body together is snapped. Matthew Henry, in his classic commentary on the Bible says, "Man is a strange sort of creature, a ray of heaven united to a clod of earth; at death these are separated and each goes to the place whence it came. The body, that clod of clay, returns to its own earth. The soul, that beam of light, returns to that God who, when he made man of the dust of the ground, breathed into him the breath of life, to make him a living soul." (Gen 2:7)[1]

At death, the water of life that used to flow from the pitcher into the "golden bowl of life," ceases to flow. The wheel of life inside our bodies, that caused all our cells and vessels and arteries to carry life to each part of the body, now is broken like a spring inside a watch. Man's body, now no longer needed as his earth suit, returns to dust from whence it was made. Paul reminds us in I Corinthians 15:44 that in death "It is sown a natural body; it is raised a spiritual body."

Solomon, the Preacher, preaches his final sermon titled "Remember your Creator NOW…be faithful NOW!" For those who are young and say, "I'll get serious about God later," what about all the "baggage" you will bring along because you waited? He is saying don't get the point of being in a nursing home with fear of death, wondering, "What did I do with my life? Am I ready for eternity?" Solomon is saying, "Walk by faith and be faithful now so that when you are aged and near death, you are not fearful but rather full of peace and joy, knowing you are going 'home.'"

Read I Corinthians 15:54-57.

54 When the perishable puts on the imperishable, and the mortal puts on immortality, then shall come to pass the saying that is written: "Death is swallowed up in victory." 55 "O death, where is your victory? O death, where is your sting?" 56 The sting of death is sin, and the power of sin is the law. 57 But thanks be to God, who gives us the victory through our Lord Jesus Christ.

What brings about victory over death?

Read Matthew 6:25 and 31-33.

25 "Therefore I tell you, do not be anxious about your life, what you will eat or what you will drink, nor about your body, what you will put on. Is not life more than food, and the body more than clothing?

31 Therefore do not be anxious, saying, 'What shall we eat?' or 'What shall we drink?' or 'What shall we wear?' 32 For the Gentiles seek after all these things, and your heavenly Father knows that you need them all. 33 But seek first the kingdom of God and his righteousness, and all these things will be added to you.

✺ What should we worry about?

✺ What should we focus on?

Solomon ends his sermon the way he started by describing life on earth. Remember, he took us on a journey in a spiral starting at the bottom of life with the message, "Meaningless! Meaningless! Everything is meaningless!" He concludes, "Remember your Creator" now while you have time. This is Solomon's final plea as he ends his message.

Solomon discovered with all of his supernatural wisdom that life "under the sun" without God is meaningless vanity. However, when we are committed to God and grow in spiritual maturity and intimacy with Christ, we can go from glory to glory and have the joy and fulfillment of bearing "much fruit" as we serve Him faithfully to the end. This is the joy of the Winter Season!

[1]*Commentary on the Whole Bible by Matthew Henry,* Edited by Rev. Leslie F Church, Phd., Zondervan Publish House, Grand Rapids, Michigan, 1961.

A Bit of Wisdom

Solomon's gloomy picture of old age does not negate the truth that old age can be blessed for the godly. Proverbs 16:31 says, *"Gray hair is a crown of glory; it is gained in a righteous life."* Old age" can be glorious! It can truly feel like the "golden years" as you have more freedom with your time. One of the joys you can have is praying regularly for your children and grandchildren, so they will be prepared for life in service to Christ. Praying with your mate or a prayer partner forms a special bond, and you'll be closer than ever before. Life can keep getting sweeter!

What is the Answer to Life Under the Sun?

Day 5

Father God, I praise You for Who you are, the Creator of heaven and earth, the God of all gods and Lord of all lords. Search me, O God, and know my heart! Test me, and know my thoughts and see if there is anything offensive in me, and lead me in the way everlasting. I pray that Your Word would be a lamp to my feet and a light to my path. Thank You for all that You have done for me. I love You, Lord. In Jesus' name I pray. Amen.

Her family knew that Elizabeth had very little time left on this earth. Her body was frail. Breathing, eating, and standing were becoming almost impossible. As her grandchildren gathered at her bedside, she spoke softly to them. "Children, life is so brief and fragile. Be careful with the way you live your life. Spend your time worshiping our Father, spend your energy advancing God's kingdom while you're still young, and spend this life loving others sacrificially and with a pure heart. My prayer for you is that you will live a rich and full life, loving God with all your heart, soul, mind, and strength and that you will love the people of this world as you make an impact on the nations for Jesus Christ.

I want you to really enjoy your lives. Life is so beautiful. You'll make important choices: who to marry, how to build your future careers, how to spend your minutes, days, weeks, and years. There is a time for everything in its season. Your life is before you, and you only have one to live. Live it well! If you will love God with all your heart and spend your life loving your neighbor as you love yourself, you will have real, true joy. I love you and I'll be waiting in heaven for you." She closed her eyes, and the grandchildren quietly left her room. With her sisters gathered around her, Elizabeth kept her appointment with her Savior only a few days later.

Read Ecclesiastes 12:9-12.

What did you learn about Solomon's spiritual gifts in these verses?

Do you think Solomon, the Preacher, found words of delight in writing Ecclesiastes?

What did you find "delightful" about Ecclesiastes?

How are words like nails or goads?

How was Solomon feeling about the writing process?

Solomon probably wrote the book of Ecclesiastes in his final years. He had the spiritual gift of teaching, besides the gifts of preaching and discernment, and he used his gifts to systematically share all that he had learned. He wrote his books in a way that others could receive and understand God's wisdom by writing most of his instruction in short proverbs that were easy to remember. Even in his circular, spiraling book of Ecclesiastes, he used the teaching method of repetition to go over and over his lessons for his students. He wrote truth in a way simple people could comprehend by using universal illustrations common to all in concise "sound bites" of information.

Verse 10 sounds a bit surprising. Did Solomon really seek to find "words of delight" to impart truth? Most people reading Ecclesiastes wouldn't say it's a delightful book! But Solomon wants us to "feel our way" through Ecclesiastes rather than "reason our way." This is what he has been saying for 12 chapters: All that you see "under the sun" is not all there is. There is more, MUCH more to life "above the sun" that includes joy, wisdom, and faith. Solomon seeks to teach us what he has learned the hard way: The words of truth are sometimes like goads.

My husband, David, grew up around sheep and cattle, and he has taught me about the use of a goad on a ranch. A goad is a sharp stick, or nowadays an electric prod, to guide farm animals to go in a certain direction. But if the animal is obstinate, he may "kick against the goad." The result is pain. Solomon gives words of wisdom to prod us to go a certain way; and if we rebel against them, we will pay the consequences.

These words are also like nails in that they hold things together. They're meant to cause permanent, transformative change in our lives. And most importantly, they're inspired by one Shepherd, the Lord Jesus. The word "shepherd" isn't used anywhere else in the book of Ecclesiastes, but Solomon must have known "the Lord as his shepherd" taught to him by his father, David, who wrote Psalm 23. Solomon understood that he may be a *conduit* of truth but that the Lord is the ultimate shepherd for His sheep to *know* the truth.

Solomon then gives a commentary on the act of writing. "Under the sun" mankind is constantly writing new books to share new knowledge. According to the annual Bowker Report, in the United States alone, more than a million books are published each year. Many of these books probably aren't necessary, and most will be irrelevant and forgotten by next year. But the one book that stands the test of time and truth is the Word of God, the Bible. It is a supernatural book. Hebrews 4:12 tells us, *"For the word of God is living and active, sharper than any two-edged sword, piercing to the division of soul and spirit, of joints and marrow, and discerning the thoughts and intentions of the heart."*

Finally, Solomon is ready to give us the "punch line"—his final thesis for this wisdom book.

Read Ecclesiastes 12:13, 14.
^{13}The end of the matter; all has been heard. Fear God and keep his commandments, for this is the whole duty of man. ^{14}For God will bring every deed into judgment, with every secret thing, whether good or evil.

✳ What is Solomon's final conclusion to his search for meaning and purpose in life?

✳ What does it mean to "fear God?"

✳ What would be the wrong interpretation of "fear God?"

✳ Why should we keep God's commandments and fear Him?

With his brilliant mind, Solomon openly and honestly searched out the meaning of life to find out, "Why are we here?" This search continues in the world today. The British atheistic philosopher, Bertrand Russell, coined an interesting phrase in his 1929 essay, "A Free Man's Worship" when he wrote, "…life must only be built on the firm foundation of unyielding despair." Later, he said, "The secret to happiness is to face the fact that the world is horrible, horrible, horrible.[2] Unfortunately, Russell, like many today, stopped short of finding life's true meaning. If you only look at the pain and suffering of this world, you will despair. But Solomon's wisdom took him to the truth.

He has drawn a line on the horizon and tests life below it. He is the scientist who has examined life apart from God, faith, and the supernatural; and he also observes life God's way. Solomon, perhaps the only person who ever lived who was able to experience ALL that life has to offer "under the sun," can tell us with accuracy which way works best. He tried money (billions) and pleasure (700 wives and 300 concubines!) and work (He built the most important building in the world—the Temple) and explored science, philosophy, and psychology to find the ultimate meaning of life. Then, he turned around to tell us that after all he's experienced, he now knows the best way to spend our lives; and he knows what to avoid. He's travelled down the road of life ahead of us and gives us a shockingly simple solution that is beautifully complex at the same time.

Here is the "end of the matter." This is what we have been waiting for…THE ultimate purpose and THE secret to a truly successful life. "Fear God and keep His commandments." Boom! There it is. The answer to life for anyone in any culture living at any time.

First, Solomon tells us to "fear God." This "fear" is not to cower before Him, but is a reverent submission, embracing the truth that God is God and we are not. It's bowing the knee, bowing the heart before God in awe of who He is. It is to take seriously the sovereignty of Almighty God.

The second part of the secret of life is to keep God's commandments. A Jewish boy like Solomon, the son of a king of Israel, would have been taught the commandments of God given to Moses in his forty days on Mt. Sinai. He would have memorized the Ten Commandments and would have been schooled in the law as written in the first five books of the Bible, the Pentateuch. We have to remember that he was an Old Testament man living under the Old Covenant of the law, and at that time, those laws were the only path for coming into the covenant promises of God. It's understandable that his exhortation at the end of his book is to tell us to keep the law. But we have the rest of the story.

Both Solomon and Jesus tell us the secret to life, but instead of the law, Jesus brings grace. Where Solomon concluded that the best we can do is to, *"Fear God,"* Jesus said, *"LOVE the Lord your God with all your heart and with all your soul and with all your mind and with all your strength."* Where Solomon said, *"Keep His commandments,"* Jesus' message took us beyond obedience to love. In John 14:15, He said "if you LOVE Me, keep My commandments." He summarized the Old Testament commandments by telling us it's not about our behavior; it's all about relationship. The commandment is to LOVE our neighbor as ourself. Solomon takes us in the right direction, but Jesus leads us home.

Read I John 4:16-18.

¹⁶So we have come to know and to believe the love that God has for us. God is love, and whoever abides in love abides in God, and God abides in him. ¹⁷By this is love perfected with us, so that we may have confidence for the day of judgment, because as he is, so also are we in this world. ¹⁸ here is no fear in love, but perfect love casts out fear. For fear has to do with punishment, and whoever fears has not been perfected in love.

Fill in the blank:

"God is _____ and whoever abides in _____ abides in God and God abides in him.

"There is no _____ in love, but perfect _____ casts out _____."

My mother taught me that God isn't just loving, nice, and kind. He's not just a benevolent Father, although He is all of those things. She said, "Honey, God IS love. That is who He is. It is the essence of His nature and cannot be separated from Him. It is a law of the universe. God is love. It's not what He does; it is who He is. All true love comes from Him."

Our relationship with God isn't based on the law; it's all based on love. Jesus not only kept the commandments as He walked the earth, He paid the penalty for us when we don't. We have abundant life, not because we pursue pleasure, work, and wealth but because Jesus loves us.

We can't fear or love God on our own. We can't keep His commandments by loving our neighbors as ourselves in our own strength. Jesus does this for us. He gave up His life so His can pour through ours. When we surrender completely to Him, He will do it all for us, in us, and through us. Only then can we do as Solomon says to "fear" and love God. Only then can we keep His commandments by loving our neighbors as ourselves.

Solomon closes his book on a somber note. After he gives us the ultimate way to live our lives by fearing and obeying God, he sends us a parting warning. It almost sounds like he finishes his sermon, steps down from the pulpit, and as he walks away, I can almost hear him saying to himself under his breath the words of Ecclesiastes 12:14. *"For God will bring every deed into judgment, with every secret thing, whether good or evil."*

Solomon knew there would be a reckoning day, and he dreaded it. God had given him specific instructions at the beginning of his reign in I Kings 3:14. *"And if you will walk in my ways, keeping my statutes and my commandments, as your father David walked, then I will lengthen your days."* God's commands to a king of Israel was to marry within the covenant and not take a foreign wife. Solomon disobeyed this command 1000 times! I Kings 11:4 says, *"For when Solomon was old his wives turned away his heart after other gods, and his heart was not wholly true to the Lord his God, as was the heart of David his father."*

He looks back at his life and sees the cost of his disobedience. God gave him every chance for an amazing life, and it was derailed by foolish and rebellious choices. Solomon now realized that because there is a God in heaven, everything we do matters—including the actions of a king. He was at the end of life facing the consequences of disobedience, and it left him with bitter regret. He trembled at a day of judgment when he would be called to account for his deeds. John tells us in I John 4:17, 18, *"By this is love perfected with us, so that we may have confidence for the day of judgment, because as he is, so also are we in this world. ⁱ⁸There is no fear in love, but perfect love casts out fear. For fear has to do with punishment, and whoever fears has not been perfected in love."* Those of us who have given our lives to Christ and received His love, forgiveness, and salvation have nothing to fear. We have been saved from the penalty of sin and now have eternal life; there is no condemnation. Romans 8:1 says, *"There is therefore now no condemnation for those who are in Christ Jesus."* We are accountable for our actions, but we are not condemned.

The overarching purpose of this book is that life "under the sun" really is meaningless without God. You can try money, power, sex, and work to find meaning in your life, but like Solomon, you'll only end in regret. He discovered when all is said and done that it is only a life of obedient faith in God "above the sun" that gives it purpose and meaning. Solomon may have made foolish mistakes, but remember that he's still the wisest man who ever lived. He gives us counsel on how to find a good work-life balance, how to save and spend our money, how to leave a legacy, and finally, how to live joyfully! Solomon knows only to tell us to fear and obey God. Jesus invites us into a love relationship because God isn't just loving; God IS love. The choice is ours, especially in a Winter Season; will we walk away from or toward that love?

[1]bible-studys.org
[2]*Bertrand Russell, the Passionate Sceptic,* Alan Wood, 1957, pp. 236-7.

A Personal Message from Denise

Dear Reader,

I'm right there with you in my Winter Season, and I need these words of wisdom from Ecclesiastes. Winter seasons aren't easy and often do feel that all is meaningless; but after studying Ecclesiastes, it has helped me navigate times of grief, times of joy and even the aging process. It has encouraged me to remain faithful to the end and press in even more to Jesus.

I pray that you will find comfort and encouragement in your Winter Season and that these words of wisdom from Ecclesiastes will bring transformation in your life as you choose to live "above the sun."

Hearts Surrendered. Lives Transformed.

KARDO MINISTRIES

- Visit our website, www.kardo.org to connect with our ministry community.
- Get to know Denise and David Glenn
- Sign up for our email newsletter
- Find more resources for your Bible study group
- Discover a global prayer team
- Stay current on upcoming events

If you're looking for Bible studies in Spanish, Korean, Russian, Mandarin, German, Kiswahili, Vietnamese, Indonesian, or other languages, visit our website www.kardo.org where you'll find *Wisdom for Mothers*, *Wisdom for Fathers*, *Restore My Heart*, and other studies wonderfully translated with easy to use DVD's and leader's guides. Consider these for your next mission trip!

www.kardo.org
888-272-6972

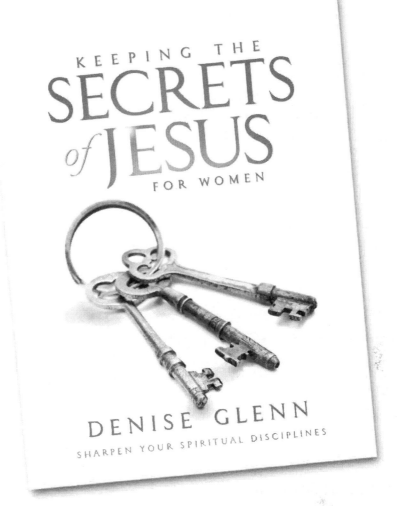

If you are looking for a Bible study tht will take spirtual growth to a new level, then **Keeping the Secrets of Jesus for Women** is what you have been searching for!

Denise has taken the amazing original study and revised it in workbook format to focus on the challenges that women face today and how to deal with those challanges using spiritual Disciplines. In this 6 week study women will learn how to:
- Pray in ways that will demolish strongholds
- Give sacrificially and effectively
- Fast in an effort to draw near God
- Use worship as a weapon to fight spiritual battles
- Engage your faith as never before

Using Matthew 6 and lessons learned while living overseas, Denise will take women through a life changing studying of the Secrets that jesus taught. Your spiritual skills and disciplines will be sharpened and taked to new depths for a deeper relationship with God.

Bible study lessons are on DVD and leader discussion questions are located at the end of the workbook.

Available now online! Visit www.kardo.org or call 1-888-272-6972.

Restore My Heart

Learn how to have your heart restored to the function of its original design, transporting God's love to you, through you, and to others!

Explore God's Word in this penetrating 6-week Bible study about Christ's love for you and His invitation to you! Discover the passion of the Lord God for His people; how tenderly and compassionately you are loved, just as you are; and His desire to lavishly adorn you with His precious gifts.

• Find out how these eternal truths are beautifully illustrated for today's women in the ancient Jewish customs and wedding traditions.

• Learn from Denise how a toothbrush, a pickle, and heavenly sand paper can illuminate God's Word in your life.

• Receive healing and restoration as you bring your hurting and wounded heart to the One Who made the ultimate sacrifice for His Bride, the Church.

RESTORE MY HEART DVD SET:
Taped-live sessions with Denise Glenn teaching the Bible study content of the workbook

RESTORE MY HEART CD SET:
The audio portion of Denise Glenn's video series is available in a 3-CD holder.

RESTORE MY HEART LEADER'S GUIDE:
Complete instructions for leading *Restore My Heart* in a large or small group setting whether in a church or home.

"A thoughtful reading of "Restore My Heart" will provide fresh in-sight to readers as the author makes a vivid comparison of the Jewish wedding traditions with our heritage as the Bride of Christ. Our identity in Him and His unconditional love for us give ample cause for rejoicing in 'so great salvation' (Hebrews. 2:3)."

Charles R. Solomon, Author, "Handbook to Happiness".

"In 'Restore My Heart' Denise Glenn reminds us that as Christians, we are the love of the Lord's life! Through Jesus' teaching of Himself as the Bridegroom and the Church as the Bride, Denise brings the reader and the Lord together for an inspirational and intimate visit and study of that unique and fulfilling relationship."

H. Edwin Young, Senior Pastor, Second Baptist Church, Houston, TX

Freedom for Mothers

As mothers, it is our heart's desire to be loving and joyful, full of peace and patience in relating to our families. Unfortunately, there is often a Grand Canyon: between our hopes and reality.

The Freedom For Mothers Workbook Helps You:

· Find the source to fill your "love bucket"

· Recognize common mothering traps

· Deal decisively with self-defeating habits in mothering

· Let Christ's love and patience flow through you to your family

· Experience God's peace in your mothering circumstances

In addition, you'll be equipped with mothering skills to help you set appropriate boundaries for your children. You'll understand how to take appropriate steps in guiding your children through the progressive stages of maturity, and even to "letting go" when the time comes.

Freedom for Mothers DVD Set: Taped sessions with Denise Glenn teaching the Bible Study content of the workbook, including material for the introductory session and mothering skills.

Freedom for Mothers Audio: The audio portion of Denise Glenn's video series is available in CDs.

Freedom for Mothers Leader's Guide: Complete instructions for leading *Freedom for Mothers* in a MotherWise group setting.

"Mothering is just about the hardest job around. Denise's materials put powerful tools into the hands of mothers to navigate the journey victoriously."

—*Josh McDowell, speaker and author*

Materials available: workbooks, DVD lessons, CDs, and leader's guides.
Order Today! www.kardo.org   1-888-272-6972

MotherWise is a lifeline for mothers of all ages and stages providing the biblical and practical instruction moms need to thrive in today's chaotic, changing world. Denise Glenn's Bible Study materials will take you deep into "God's Word to find the answers you seek to rear godly offspring and build a solid marriage. MotherWise is more than materials…it is a community of mothers networking to pray for and nourish each other in the high calling of motherhood.

Wisdom for Mothers

Wisdom for Mothers can help you find Biblical answers for your important parenting questions.

You'll learn to bring order to your life when you discover the truth about:

· Your Relationship With God—Learning To Trust And Obey
· Your Relationship With Your Husband—What About Submission?
· Your Relationship With Your Children—Settling Your Questions About Discipline
· Your Relationship With Work—Four Biblical Tests For A Woman's Daily Work
· Your Relationship With The World—Having A Heart For Service

You'll learn practical mothering skills:
- How To Have A Quiet Time When It's Never Quiet At Your House
- Discipline Techniques That Work
- Food For The Whole Family
- Getting your Family Organized
- Romancing The Home
- How To Have Family Night Without Chaos

Wisdom for Mothers materials include: workbook, DVDs, CDs, and leader's guides. For more information visit www.kardo.org.

"Are you a mom who needs encouragement, hope, energy? WISE up! Let Denise show you the way through her teaching and heartwarming stories."
—Dr. Kevin Leman, author of The Birth Order Book

"These materials give excellent encouragement to mothers who are in the middle of raising a family. Thanks, Denise, for pointing moms back to Christ to find the strength and wisdom they need to meet life head on."
—Dennis Rainey, Family Life Today, Campus Crusade for Christ

"Denise Glenn has a gift for helping to bring God's Word of truth alive for today's women. Her warm and engaging style welcomes you into the very essence of God's encompassing love and provision. Join her for this journey into healing, hope, encouragement and the call of God's heart of love for you." - L.B.

"The series MotherWise is the best material I have ever seen on mothering. Wisdom for Mothers gives practical advice on the everyday work of mothering. It is thoroughly scriptural and covers all facets of what most mothers worry about. Mrs. Glenn is frank about the real problems mothers face, with insightful, biblical advice on how to meet the problems. I recommend these books to all mothers who have Christian concern for godly practice."
—Dr. T. W. Hunt, professor, author of The Mind of Christ, the Doctrine of Prayer, Disciple's Prayer Life

"Denise invites you to encounter God on mountaintops–and enjoy His glory. Denise has been my prayer partner for years. She loves to pray, and she has a huge heart for worship. She created 'Fan the Flame' to help you scale the heights of worship!"   —Sarah Young, author of "Jesus Calling"

Fan the Flame

Discover Worship on the Mountains of the Bible That Will Fire Up Your Passion for God.

Speaker and author, Denise Glenn, will take you on a journey to learn more about worship on six different mountaintops in Scripture. When fire and mountains come together, God teaches His people something new about worship—something they didn't know before. If you are hungry for revival, hungry to hear God's voice and ready to see God at work, *Fan the Flame* is for you. Leader's Guides, DVD sets, and CD sets available to accompany this bible study pupil's workbook.

...fan into flame the gift of God which is in you... 2 Timothy 1:6

Denise Glenn is a mom, grandmother, author, popular speaker, and co-founder of Kardo Ministries. She speaks to women on topics from her books, **Keeping the Secrets of Jesus, Restore My Heart, Wisdom for Mothers,** and **Freedom for Mothers**. Denise began MotherWise, a discipleship ministry for wives and mothers, in 1981 when she had three preschoolers. From a small group of five women, the ministry of MotherWise has grown to reach women around the world with discipleship materials in their own heart languages. Today, with her materials translated into 11 languages, Denise's global teaching ministry reaches beyond mothers to include women of all ages and stages. She has been featured on many American radio broadcasts including, "Revive Our Hearts" with Nancy Leigh DeMoss, "Family Life Today" with Dennis Rainey, and Josh McDowell's nationwide program. She is sought out as a speaker for women's events both nationally and internationally.

Denise and her husband, David, are co-founders of Kardo Ministries, a non-profit international organization providing bible study and mentoring materials and conferences. Kardo materials authored by the Glenn's cover the deeper aspects of Christian family life and discipleship such as covenant marriage, rearing godly children, worship, prayer, fasting, giving, and our identity in Christ. David and Denise have taught these materials in conferences in the United States, as well as in Australia, New Zealand, Botswana, Kenya, Malaysia, Indonesia, Singapore, Korea, the Philippines, China, Vietnam, Germany, Austria, Ukraine, Russia, Belarus, Costa Rica and Nicaragua. They enlist powerful prayer warriors to pray before, during, and following each event.

www.kardo.org
1-888-272-6972